The Pizza Tastes Great Workbook

William P. Pickett
Passaic High School

PRENTICE HALL REGENTS

Acquisitions Editor: Nancy Baxer
Director of Production and Manufacturing: David Riccardi
Editorial Production/Design Manager: Dom Mosco
Production Editors and Compositors: Michael J. Bertrand and Wanda Espana
Cover Design/Interior Art Coordinator: Merle Krumper
Cover Design: Wanda Espana
Illustrations by: Richard Toglia
Electronic Art: Peter Ticola
Production Coordinator: Ray Keating

Printed in the United States of America
10 9

ISBN 0-13-102492-2

To My Mother and Father

Contents

Preface

Purpose

The purpose of *The Pizza Workbook* is to reinforce what students have learned from the dialogues and stories of *The Pizza Tastes Great*, and to provide the students with new dialogues and stories and with exercises that foster a creative and independent use of English.

Content

All eight chapters of *The Pizza Workbook* begin with a review section. This section consists of true-false questions to check the student's comprehension of a dialogue or story of *The Pizza Tastes Great* and sentence completion exercises to test and reinforce the vocabulary of *The Pizza*.

A new dialogue or story follows the review section. The new dialogues are patterned on the original ones, but feature new ideas and new vocabulary. After the students complete the new dialogue, they either write a dialogue of their own or they interview another student or some other person. In writing their own dialogues, they use the dialogues of *The Pizza* and *The Pizza Workbook* as models.

The new stories are shorter and easier than those in *The Pizza Tastes Great* and are meant to be read and enjoyed and to serve as models for student compositions.

Each lesson, therefore, progresses from a review section to a new dialogue or story, to sections in which the students apply what they have learned by writing their own dialogue and story or by interviewing. This gives the students the opportunity to be creative and to express their own ideas. The language they produce will be imperfect, but their self-activity will help develop confidence and an ability to use English independently.

Use

The exercises is this workbook can be used immediately after completing a dialogue or story in *The Pizza*, or they can be used to review a chapter after it has been completed. The workbook, of course, can be used in class or at home.

Word List, Chapter Tests, and Answer Key

In the back of the workbook there is a word list. A separate booklet contains a one-page vocabulary test for each chapter of *The Pizza Tastes Great* and an answer key for the workbook and chapter tests.

Field-Testing

This workbook was originally field-tested in the author's classes at the Passaic Adult Learning Center. The workbook has also been field-tested at Passaic High School by the author and others. One of the teachers wrote of it, "By the way, we are really enjoying this workbook. It is a very valuable addition to the book."

Acknowledgments

I wish to thank Nancy Baxer, Nancy Leonhardt, Anne Riddick, and Jack Ross of Prentice Hall Regents for their assistance and encouragement in writing *The Pizza Workbook*. I would also like to thank Dom Mosco, Wanda España, Michael Bertrand, and Merle Krumper of Prentice Hall Regents for the part they played in its production.

I am grateful to Mrs. Audrey Seidner and the other teachers at Passaic High School who helped field-test this text.

Finally, I thank my wife Dorothy for her help and suggestions in reviewing *The Pizza Workbook*.

1

Food

Review

Reread the dialogue **A Good Cook** *(page 2 of* **The Pizza Tastes Great***) before doing the dialogue and word reviews.*

I. Dialogue Review

If the sentence is true, write **T**. *If it's false, write* **F** *and change it to a true statement.*

_____   1. Mario is in the living room.

_____

_____   2. He's cooking dinner.

_____

_____   3. His wife is watching the children.

_____

_____   4. She's tired.

_____

_____   5. She can cook.

_____

_____   6. Mario isn't a good cook.

_____

II. Word Review

Complete the sentences with these words.

where's	**kitchen**	**cook**	**dinner**

1. I'm hungry. Is _____ ready?

2. The cat is in the _____.

3. _____ my hat?

4. I like to _____.

tired	**wife**	**watching**	**can**

5. I'm _____. I want to sit down.

6. _____ Pablo speak English?

7. Who is _____ the baby?

8. Your _____ is pretty.

On the Phone

Listen to and pronounce these words.

	Nouns		**Verbs**	**Other**
dining room	daughter		eat	much
dinner	phone		talk	

Complete the dialogue with these words and practice it with your partner.

daughter   all   dining room   talking   much   eating

Wing: Where's Chen?

 Lee: He's in the _____.

Wing: What's he doing?

 Lee: He's _____ dinner with his wife.

Wing: Where's his _____?

 Lee: In the kitchen.

Wing: What's she doing?

 Lee: _____ on the phone.

Wing: Is she on the phone _____?

 Lee: Yes, _____ the time.

Writing a Dialogue

Work with a partner and create your own dialogue. Use the words in this lesson and other words you know.

_____

A: Where's _____?

B. She's _____.

A: What's she doing?

B: _____

A: _____

B: _____

A: _____

B: _____

Rooms in a House

List as many rooms as you can that are in a house. Then list two things you see in them.

Rooms	**Two Things in Them**
1. _____	_____
2. _____	_____
3. _____	_____
4. _____	_____
5. _____	_____
6. _____	_____
7. _____	_____
8. _____	_____

Review

Reread the dialogue **We Eat a Lot** *(page 6 of* **The Pizza Tastes Great***) before doing the dialogue and word review.*

I. Dialogue Review

If the sentence is true, write **T**. *If it's false, write* **F** *and change it to a true statement.*

_____ 1. The car keys are on the dining room table.

_____

_____ 2. Terry is going to the bank.

_____

_____ 3. Terry and Chris eat a lot.

_____

_____ 4. Terry wants Chris to go with her.

_____

_____ 5. Chris is busy.

_____

_____ 6. The packages will be heavy.

_____

II. Word Review

Complete the sentences with these words.

will   **if**   **again**   **key**

1. Where's the _____ to the cabinet?

2. I _____ see you tomorrow.

3. Say it _____.

4. _____ you need help, ask me.

packages   **a lot**   **heavy**   **busy**

5. Henry talks _____.

6. Put the _____ on the table.

7. Is the store _____ on Saturday morning?

8. These books are _____.

Baseball in the Park

Listen to and pronounce these words.

Nouns	**Verbs**	**Other**
sweater	play	too
park	use	another

Complete the dialogue with these words and practice it with your partner.

play   **sweater**   **another**   **living room**   **too**   **park**

Pat: Did you see my _____?

Jay: It's in the _____.

Pat: You're right. Thanks.

Jay: Where are you going?

Pat: To the _____.

Jay: Again?

Pat: Yes, I love to _____ baseball.

Jay: Can I go with you?

Pat: Sure you can.

Jay: I like to play baseball, _____.

Pat: Good. We can use _____ player.

Interviewing

Ask your partner or some other person these questions.

1. May I ask you some questions?

2. Do you like to talk on the phone?

3. Do you ever call another country? Which country? Do you call it much?

4. Do you like baseball?

5. Do you ever watch it on TV?

6. Do you have a team you like very much? If you do, what team?

7. Do they play baseball in your first country? Much?

8. Can you name two countries, and not the United States, that love baseball?

What I Like to Do

List some things you like to do.

1. I like to _____.

2. I like to _____.

3. I like to _____.

4. I like to _____.

Places I Go

List some places you go to.

1. I go to _____.

2. I go to _____.

3. I go to _____.

4. I go to _____.

Review

Reread the dialogue **A Little Milk but No Sugar** *(page 9 of* **The Pizza Tastes Great***) before doing the dialogue and word reviews.*

I. Dialogue Review

If the sentence is true, write **T**. *If it's false, write* **F** *and change it to a true statement.*

_____   1. Gerry wants a cup of coffee.

_____

_____   2. Gerry asks for a little milk and sugar.

_____

_____   3. Carol frequently drinks coffee at night.

_____

_____   4. Coffee keeps Carol awake.

_____

_____   5. Tea helps Carol relax.

_____

_____   6. Gerry loves tea.

_____

II. Word Review

Complete the sentences with these words.

at night   **never**   **please**   **something**

1. I have _____ to give you.

2. Open the door, _____.

3. Igor doesn't like to drive _____.

4. Ann _____ goes to the movies.

little   **relax**   **awake**   **keep**

5. Stay _____ in class!

6. This coat will _____ me warm.

7. Come in, sit down, and _____.

8. May I have a _____ more ice cream?

I Love Cake

Listen to and pronounce these words.

Nouns		Verbs	Other
chocolate	apple	would	hot
piece	orange		me too
cake	fruit		any
dessert			too

Complete the dialogue with these words and practice it with your partner.

any　　**too**　　**like**　　**piece**　　**dessert**　　**chocolate**

Sandy: Would you _____ something to drink?

Robin: A cup of hot _____, please.

Sandy: And a _____ of cake?

Robin: Sure, I love cake.

Sandy: Me too, but I can't have _____ .

Robin: Why not?

Sandy: I'm _____ heavy.

Robin: What do you eat for _____?

Sandy: An apple or an orange.

Robin: I don't like fruit for dessert.

Writing a Dialogue

Work with a partner and create your own dialogue. Use the words in this lesson and other words you know.

_____

A:　Would you like something to drink?

B:　_____, please.

A:　And　_____?

B:　Sure, I　_____.

A:　_____

B:　_____

A:　_____

B:　_____

Drinks, Desserts, Fruits

Work with a partner and try to list eight drinks, desserts, and fruits. Put a check (√) after those that you like a lot.

Drinks	Desserts	Fruits
1.		
2.		
3.		
4.		
5.		
6.		
7.		
8.		

Review

Reread the dialogue **A Big Menu** *(page 12 of* **The Pizza Tastes Great***) before doing the dialogue and word reviews.*

I. Dialogue Review

If the sentence is true, write **T**. *If it's false, write* **F** *and change it to a true statement.*

_____ 1. The restaurant has a small menu.

_____

_____ 2. Jackie is getting turkey, peas, and mashed potatoes.

_____

_____ 3. The fish at the restaurant isn't good.

_____

_____ 4. Fran had fish yesterday.

_____

_____ 5. Fran gets roast beef and a baked potato.

_____

_____ 6. Fran likes vegetables.

_____

II. Word Review

Complete the sentence with these words.

menu	**getting**	**perfect**	**vegetables**

1. Eat your _____! They're good for you.

2. Waiter! May I have a _____, please.

3. No one is _____.

4. I'm _____ soup and a salad for lunch.

fish	**any**	**how about**	**baked**

5. We don't have _____ money.

6. Doug likes _____ chicken.

7. _____ a little wine before dinner?

8. I'm making a tuna _____ sandwich.

Chicken and Rice

Listen to and pronounce these words.

Nouns		**Verbs**	**Other**
steak	rice	order	pretty
french fries	carrots		excellent
salad	idea		ready
chicken			tomorrow

Complete the dialogue with these words and practice it with your partner.

tomorrow   **pretty**   **order**   **excellent**   **idea**   **ready**

Chris: This is a _____ restaurant.

Terry: Yes, and the food is _____.

Chris: Are you _____ to order?

Terry: Yes, I'm getting steak, french fries, and a salad.

Chris: I don't know what to _____.

Terry: They have very good Italian food.

Chris: No, I'm having spaghetti _____.

Terry: How about chicken?

Chris: Good _____. I'll get chicken and rice.

Terry: And what vegetable do you want?

Chris: Carrots. I love them, and they're good for me.

12

Interviewing

Ask your partner or some other person these questions.

1. May I ask you some questions?

2. What do you drink at breakfast? And at dinner?

3. Do you like hot chocolate? Do you drink much?

4. Do you like spaghetti?

5. Do you like pizza?

6. Do you eat much chicken? Rice?

7. What do you eat more often - rice or potatoes?

8. Do you like steak? Do you eat much?

Completing a Story

Work with a partner and write your own story. Use the words in this lesson and other words you know. Give the story a title.

_____

My wife and I are eating dinner at a restaurant. We are looking at the

_____. My wife is getting _____

_____. And I'm getting _____

_____. My wife is going to

have _____ for dessert, but I'm not getting any because

_____.

My wife loves to eat at restaurants because _____

_____,

but we don't eat out much because _____

_____.

Review

Reread the story **The Pizza Tastes Great** *(page 15 of* **The Pizza Tastes Great***) before doing the story, word, and word and story reviews.*

I. Story Review

If the sentence is true, write **T**. *If it's false, write* **F** *and change it to a true statement.*

_____   1. Dave works fast.

_____

_____   2. He's frequently late.

_____

_____   3. Alice walks and talks slowly.

_____

_____   4. She's frequently early.

_____

_____   5. Dave likes pizza and ice cream.

_____

_____   6. He thinks about his weight a lot.

_____

_____   7. Alice never eats cake or candy.

_____

_____   8. She never thinks about her weight.

_____

II. Word Review

Complete the sentences with these words.

fast	**so**	**diet**	**pounds**

1. I'm _____ tired.

2. Dan weighs two hundred and fifty _____.

3. He's on a _____.

4. Paula drives _____.

only	careful	slowly	different

5. My son eats _____.

6. These shoes are _____ thirty-five dollars.

7. Rosa and Carlos are married, but they're from _____ countries.

8. Sandra is a good doctor. She's very _____.

III. Word and Story Review

Eating Ice Cream

Complete the conversation with these words and practice it with your partner.

late	thin	living room	calories
favorite	early	weigh	always

Alice: Where are you?

Dave: In the _____.

Alice: What are you doing?

Dave: Reading the newspaper and eating ice cream.

Alice: You're _____ eating ice cream.

Dave: Well, it's my _____ food.

Alice: I know. And that's why you _____ so much.

Dave: And you're so _____.

Alice: That's because I eat a lot of fish and vegetables.

Dave: And you never eat ice cream or cake.

Alice: Right. I watch my _____ all the time.

Dave: What time is the party tonight?

Alice: Nine o'clock. We're leaving at eight-fifteen.

Dave: Why so _____?

Alice: I don't want to be _____.

Dave: Okay, early bird. I'll be ready.

Roger and Sam

Read and enjoy the story about Roger and Sam. Then write a similar story about Pat and Fran.

     Roger and Sam are good friends, but they're very different. Roger is tall and has blonde hair and blue eyes. Sam is short and has black hair and brown eyes. Roger is thin; Sam is fat.

     Sam and Roger also like to do different things. Sam likes to read, and he goes to the library a lot. Roger doesn't read much, and he never goes to the library. Sam likes Italian food and eats a lot. Roger likes French food, but he doesn't eat much. Sam is a great cook. Roger never cooks. Sam and Roger are very different, but they're great friends.

Pat and Fran

Work with a partner and write a story about Pat and Fran, two people who are very different. Use the words in this lesson and other words you know.

Pat and Fran are good friends, but they're very different. Pat is _____
_____. Fran is _____
_____. Pat _____
_____. Fran _____
_____.

     Pat and Fran also like to do different things. Pat likes to _____
_____. Fran likes
to _____. Pat _____
_____. Fran _____
_____.

Review

Reread the story **Alice Loves to Shop and Talk** *(page 18 of* **The Pizza Tastes Great***) before doing the story, word, and word and story reviews.*

I. Story Review

If the sentence is true, write **T***. If it's false, write* **F** *and change it to a true statement.*

_____ 1. Dave likes to spend money.

_____

_____ 2. Alice loves to buy new clothes and things for the house.

_____

_____ 3. Dave doesn't like to fight with his wife.

_____

_____ 4. Dave talks a lot.

_____

_____ 5. Everyone knows what Alice is thinking.

_____

_____ 6. Dave and Alice like to watch sports on TV.

_____

_____ 7. Alice likes to watch movies.

_____

_____ 8. When she's driving alone, Alice listens to the news.

_____

II. Word Review

Complete the sentences with these words.

because   **news**   **also**   **about**

1. What are you thinking _____?

2. I have some big _____.

3. Betty eats out a lot _____ she doesn't like to cook.

4. Joyce teaches history. Her husband is _____ a teacher.

friendly   **same**   **fighting**   **very**

5. Stan and Tony work in the _____ office.

6. I like Cindy. She's _____.

7. The coffee is _____ hot.

8. Are the children _____ again?

III. Word and Story Review

A New Dress and Shoes

Complete the conversation with these words and practice it with your partner.

alone   **shopping**   **clothes**   **buy**

listening   **spend**   **few**   **save**

Alice: What are you doing, dear?

Dave: I'm _____ to the news.

Alice: Do you want to go _____ with me?

Dave: When are you going?

Alice: In a _____ minutes.

Dave: No, I have a lot to do.

Alice: Okay, I'll go _____.

Dave: What are you going to _____?

Alice: A new dress and shoes.

Dave: You _____ a lot of money on _____.

Alice: Well, I want to look nice.

Dave: That's good, but we want to _____ some money, too.

Alice: Honey, I need a new dress and shoes.

Dave: Okay, okay, but don't spend too much.

Matching

In front of the words in column A, print the capital letters that are next to their definitions or descriptions in column B.

	Column A	Column B
__F__	1. relax	A. weighs a lot
_____	2. friendly	B. number one
_____	3. so	C. to keep
_____	4. save	D. a lot to do
_____	5. heavy	E. to cook in an oven
_____	6. buy	F. to take it easy
_____	7. favorite	G. very
_____	8. never	H. to give money to get
_____	9. busy	I. nice
_____	10. bake	J. at no time

Me

Complete these sentences about yourself.

1. I like to buy _____.

2. I like to listen to _____.

3. I like to save _____.

4. Sometimes I fight with _____.

5. I often think about _____.

6. I like to talk about _____.

7. Sometimes I'm late for _____.

8. I'm very _____.

2

Health

Review

Reread the dialogue **A Toothache** *(page 24 of* **The Pizza Tastes Great***) before doing the dialogue and word reviews.*

I. Dialogue Review

If the sentence is true, write **T**. *If it's false, write* **F** *and change it to a true statement.*

_____ 1. Lee asks what time it is.

_____

_____ 2. It's ten o'clock in the morning.

_____

_____ 3. Lee is early.

_____

_____ 4. He's going to the dentist.

_____

_____ 5. Pat is going to drive him there.

_____

_____ 6. Lee's toothache isn't bad.

_____

II. Word Review

Complete the sentences with these words.

time	**sure**	**there**	**o'clock**

1. Are you _____ your son is home?

2-3. The game starts at eight _____. What _____ do you want to go to the game?

4. We can walk _____.

toothache	**very**	**sorry**	**hear**

5. I'm _____ that you're sick.

6. Joe isn't going to the dance. He has a _____.

7. Can you _____ me?

8. I want something to eat. I'm _____ hungry.

Is it Bad?

Listen to and pronounce these words.

Nouns	**Other**
party	glad
headache	bad

Complete the dialogue with these words and practice it with your partner.

too   **early**   **with**   **glad**   **party**   **headache**

Terry: What time is it?

Dean: Seven-thirty.

Terry: Good. I'm _____.

Dean: Where are you going?

Terry: To a _____.

Dean: Is your wife going _____ you?

Terry: No, she has a _____.

Dean: Is it bad?

Terry: Not _____ bad.

Dean: I'm _____ to hear that.

Writing a Dialogue

Work with a partner and create your own dialogue. Use the words in this lesson and other words you know.

_____

A: What time is it?

B: _____

A: _____

B: Where are you going?

A: _____

B: _____

A: _____

B: _____

Aches

Circle how often you have these problems.

Problems	How Often I Have Them			
1. headache	frequently	sometimes	almost never	never
2. toothache	frequently	sometimes	almost never	never
3. stomachache	frequently	sometimes	almost never	never
4. earache	frequently	sometimes	almost never	never
5. I get sick	frequently	sometimes	almost never	never

Review

Reread the dialogue **Sneezing a Lot** *(page 27 of* **The Pizza Tastes Great***) before doing the dialogue and word reviews.*

I. Dialogue Review

If the sentence is true, write **T**. *If it's false, write* **F** *and change it to a true statement.*

_____ 1. Carol says she has a headache.

_____

_____ 2. She has a cold.

_____

_____ 3. She's sneezing a lot.

_____

_____ 4. Jamie hopes Carol feels better.

_____

_____ 5. Carol is taking aspirin.

_____

_____ 6. Contac keeps her awake.

_____

II. Word Review

Complete the sentences with these words.

soon   **feel**   **God**   **sleepy**

1. I _____ great. And you?

2. The bus will be here _____.

3. I'm tired and _____. It's late.

4. _____ will help us.

hope   **cold**   **every**   **better**

5. You're sneezing again. Are you getting a _____?

6. Marissa is a _____ student than Linda.

7. I _____ you like my idea.

8. Ahmad buys the newspaper _____ morning.

Do You Feel Hot?

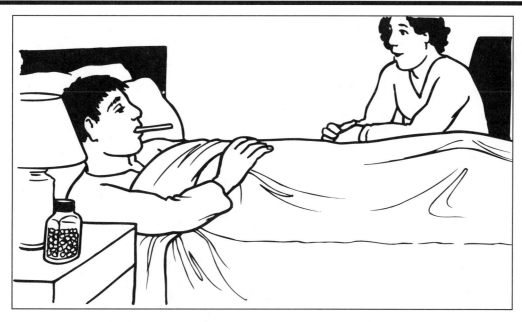

Listen to and pronounce these words.

Nouns		**Other**
temperature	aspirin	today
medicine	bit	sick

Complete the dialogue with these words and practice it with your partner.

temperature   today   bit   sick   medicine   why

Kelly: I can't go to work _____.

Tracy: _____ not?

Kelly: I'm _____.

Tracy: Do you feel hot?

Kelly: Very. My _____ is a hundred and two.

Tracy: Are you taking any _____?

Kelly: Aspirin.

Tracy: Does it help?

Kelly: A little _____.

Tracy: I hope you feel better.

Kelly: Thank you.

Interviewing

Ask your partner or some other person these questions.

1. May I ask you some questions?

2. How do you feel?

3. When you get a headache, do you take anything for it?

4. What do you take? Does it help much?

5. Can you drive?

6. Do you have a driver's license?

7. Do you like parties? A lot?

8. Do you go to many parties?

Sentence Completion

Complete these sentences.

1. I'm glad that _____.

2. I'm sorry that _____.

3. I hope that _____.

4. I'm sure that _____.

5. I'm going to _____ soon.

6. I _____ every day.

Review

Reread the dialogue **I Don't Feel Well** *(page 30 of* **The Pizza Tastes Great***) before doing the dialogue and word reviews.*

I. Dialogue Review

If the sentence is true, write **T**. *If it's false, write* **F** *and change it to a true statement.*

_____ 1. Lynn is looking for his jacket.

_____

_____ 2. He feels okay.

_____

_____ 3. He has a fever.

_____

_____ 4. He has a pain in his chest.

_____

_____ 5. He has an appointment at one-thirty.

_____

_____ 6. Lynn will see Chris later.

_____

II. Word Review

Complete the sentences with these words.

looking for   **pain**   **appointment**   **well**

1. Dennis has a _____ in his side.

2. I'm _____ my watch. Did you see it?

3. Rita isn't going to work today. She's not _____.

4. Julio has a three o'clock _____ with a lawyer.

nothing   **serious**   **fever**   **later**

5. The baby feels warm. I think he has a _____.

6. I have _____ to do.

7. Donna isn't here now. She's coming _____.

8. We like our teacher, but she's very _____.

A Pain in the Shoulder

Listen to and pronounce these words.

Nouns	**Verb**
key	sleep
shoulder	

Complete the dialogue with these words and practice it with your partner.

think   keys   shoulder   table   something   sleep

Gale: Are you looking for _____?

Stacy: Yes, my car _____.

Gale: They're on the dining room _____.

Stacy: Thanks. I'm going to the doctor.

Gale: I hope it's nothing serious.

Stacy: I don't _____ it is, but I'm not sure.

Gale: What's the problem?

Stacy: I have a pain in my _____.

Gale: Is it bad?

Stacy: Very. I can't _____ at night.

Gale: That's too bad.

Writing a Dialogue

Work with a partner and create your own dialogue. Use the words in this lesson and other words you know.

_____

A: Are you looking for something?

B: Yes, my _____.

A: They're (It's) _____.

B: Thanks. I'm _____.

A: _____

B: _____

A: _____

B: _____

Simon Says, "Touch Your _____"

Work in pairs. One student says, "Touch your nose." The other student touches his or her nose. The student continues reading from the list, but doesn't read in order. In numbers 4, 7, and 20, the student says, "Point to your . . ."

1. head
2. hair
3. nose
4. eye (point to)
5. ear
6. lip
7. teeth (point to)
8. neck
9. shoulder
10. arm
11. elbow
12. hand
13. finger
14. chest
15. stomach
16. back
17. leg
18. knee
19. ankle
20. toe (point to)

Review

*Reread the dialogue **A Sore Throat** (page 33 of **The Pizza Tastes Great**) before doing the dialogue and word reviews.*

I. Dialogue Review

*If the sentence is true, write **T**. If it's false, write **F** and change it to a true statement.*

_____   1. Fran sounds terrible.

_____

_____   2. She has a sore leg.

_____

_____   3. It hurts when she walks.

_____

_____   4. She's taking hot tea and honey.

_____

_____   5. She's going to work today.

_____

_____   6. She thinks she'll feel better tomorrow.

_____

II. Word Review

Complete the sentences with these words.

voice   **sore**   **sounds**   **terrible**

1. The pain is _____.

2. I'm going to rest my feet. They're _____.

3. The dog knows my _____. He comes when I call him.

4. The music _____ great.

stay   **so**   **should**   **hurts**

5. You _____ help your brother.

6. Don't go! _____ with me!

7. My leg _____.

8. Who says Jesse isn't a good cook? His wife says _____.

The Flu

Listen to and pronounce these words.

Nouns	**Verbs**	**Other**
flu	look	maybe
Tylenol	go back	

Complete the dialogue with these words and practice it with your partner.

taking   maybe   look   know   helping   flu

Yuri: You _____ terrible.

Nadia: I have the _____.

Yuri: You should be in bed.

Nadia: I _____. I have a fever.

Yuri: Are you _____ any medicine?

Nadia: Tylenol.

Yuri: Is the Tylenol _____?

Nadia: A little.

Yuri: When are you going back to work?

Nadia: _____ on Monday. I don't know.

Interviewing

Ask your partner or some other person these questions.

1. May I ask you some questions?

2. Do you stay home from work (or school) a lot because you're sick?

3. Do you go to a doctor much?

4. What do you think of your doctor? Is he or she excellent, very good, good, or ok?

5. What do you do if you have a fever of a hundred degrees?

6.. What do you do if you have a fever of a hundred and three degrees?

7. Did you ever have the flu? Was it bad?

8. Do you ever take Tylenol? Does it help much?

Sentence Completion

Complete these sentences.

1. I think it's a **good idea** for me to _____

_____.

2. I'm not sure what I going to do tonight. **Maybe** I'll _____

_____.

3. **Tomorrow** I'm going to _____.

4. Sometimes my _____ **hurts.**

5. I know I **should** _____.

6. When I stay home from school (work), I _____

_____.

Review

Reread the story **A Doctor** *(page 36 of* **The Pizza Tastes Great***) before doing the story, word, and word and story reviews.*

I. Story Review

If the sentence is true, write **T**. *If it's false, write* **F** *and change it to a true statement.*

_____ 1. Carmen is studying to be a lawyer.

   _____

_____ 2. She lives in New York City.

   _____

_____ 3. She's very smart.

   _____

_____ 4. Her boyfriend sells computers.

   _____

_____ 5. Her parents are from Mexico.

   _____

_____ 6. They're helping to pay her bills for medical school.

   _____

_____ 7. Carmen's father works in a store.

   _____

_____ 8. Carmen has a brother, but no sisters.

   _____

II. Word Review

Complete the sentences with these words.

salesman   **another**   **go out**   **marry**

1. We need _____ chair.

2. Kevin wants to _____ Sally, but she doesn't love him.

3. Juan is a good _____. He's friendly and likes to talk.

4. It's very cold. I don't want to _____.

travel	have to	finish	department stores

5. We'll play cards when we _____ dinner.

6. It's nice to _____ to different countries.

7. Yoshi and Peggy like to shop in big _____.

8. I _____ go to school.

III. Word and Story Review

How's Carmen Doing?

Jackie is talking to Carlos, Carmen's father.

Complete the conversation with these words and practice it with your partner.

expensive	sells	a lot	bills
graduate	single	last	smart

Jackie: How's Carmen doing?

Carlos: Fine. She's studying to be a doctor.

Jackie: That's great! She's a _____ girl.

Carlos: Yes, and she studies _____.

Jackie: When is she going to _____?

Carlos: In June. This is her _____ year.

Jackie: Is medical school very _____?

Carlos: Yes. And we're helping to pay her _____.

Jackie: Is Carmen married?

Carlos: No, she's _____, but she has a boyfriend.

Jackie: What does he do?

Carlos: He _____ computers.

Jackie: Does he make a lot of money?

Carlos: I think so.

Studying to Be a Computer Programmer

Read and enjoy the story about Gloria. Then write about your own life.

My name is Gloria, and I'm twenty. I'm from Bogotá, Colombia. I speak Spanish, but I'm also learning English. I go to Passaic County Community College in Paterson, New Jersey. I live in Paterson with my dad and younger brother. My mom and my sister, who is ten, live in Bogotá, but they're going to come to the United States next year. I will be so happy to see them again.

I'm studying to be a computer programmer. It's not easy, but that's what I want to be. Most of my classes are in the morning. I study in the afternoon, and I work as a waitress at night. It's not a great job, but I need the money. I think I'm a lucky girl. I have a lot of friends, and I like school. In a few years, I will have a good job.

An Autobiograpy

Write two paragraphs about yourself. You can use some of the ideas and words from the stories about Carmen and Gloria, but be original. Write about yourself in your own way. Your can use your name for the title.

_____

My name is _____, and I'm from _____

Review

Reread the story **She Wants to Be Herself** *(page 39 of* **The Pizza Tastes Great***)*
before doing the story, word, and word and story reviews.

I. Story Review

If the sentence is true, write **T**. *If it's false, write* **F** *and change it to a true statement.*

_____ 1. Regina talks a lot.

_____

_____ 2. She wants to be like her sister.

_____

_____ 3. She goes for long rides on her bike.

_____

_____ 4. She collects stamps.

_____

_____ 5. She gets stamps from her friends, but she never buys any.

_____

_____ 6. She wants to be a Spanish teacher.

_____

_____ 7. Some of her friends say teachers don't make a lot of money.

_____

_____ 8. She thinks money is the most important thing in life.

_____

II. Word Review

Complete the sentences with these words.

collection	belong	know about	members

1. These books _____ to the school.

2. Our club needs more _____.

3. Does your father _____ the accident?

4. Jane has a big _____ of dolls.

born	was	first	than

5. The test _____ easy.

6. Texas is larger _____ California.

7. Martin Luther King, Jr., was _____ in Atlanta, Georgia, on January 15, 1929.

8. Our _____ class is at nine o'clock.

III. Word and Story Review

Stamps for Regina

Jackie is talking to Carlos, Carmen's father.

Complete the conversation with these words and practice it with your partner.

rides	like	hobby	herself
compare	collects	angry	still

Jackie: And how's Regina doing?

Carlos: Good. She's in her third year of high school.

Jackie: She looks _____ her sister.

Carlos: Yes, but I never_____ her to Carmen.

Jackie: Why not?

Carlos: It makes her _____.

Jackie: I didn't know that.

Carlos: Yes, she wants to be _____.

Jackie: Does she _____ go for long bike _____?

Carlos: Yes, she does.

Jackie: I have some stamps for her.

Carlos: Thank you. That's nice of you.

Jackie: I know she _____ them.

Carlos: Yes, it's her favorite _____.

Jackie: That's great.

Rajesh Patel

Read and enjoy the story about Rajesh Patel. Then write about someone you know well.

My friend's name is Rajesh Patel, and he's from India. He teaches math and computer science in a large high school in Chicago. He gives a lot of homework, but the students like him because he's friendly and clear, and they learn a lot in his class. His first language is Gujarati, but he speaks English very well. Rajesh is still single and lives with his parents, but he has a girlfriend, and they plan to get married next year.

Rajesh is quiet and serious and loves music. He plays the piano well and likes to listen to classical music. Baseball is his favorite sport and mine too. Sometimes we go to watch the Chicago White Sox at their new stadium. When I have a problem, I always discuss it with Rajesh. He's friendly and smart and listens very carefully. And when he has a problem, he comes to me, and I listen and tell him what I think. He's my best friend.

My Friend

Write two paragraphs about someone you know well, about a friend or a member of your family. You can get some ideas and words from the stories about Regina and Rajesh, but your story should be different.

_____

My friend's name is _____. _____

_____

_____

_____

_____

_____

_____

_____

_____

_____

_____

_____

_____

_____

3

Birthdays

Review

Reread the dialogue **Good News** *(page 45 of* **The Pizza Tastes Great***) before doing the dialogue and word reviews.*

I. Dialogue Review

If the sentence is true, write **T.** *If it's false, write* **F** *and change it to a true statement.*

_____ 1. Pat has bad news.

_____

_____ 2. Kim is going to have a baby.

_____

_____ 3. Pat and Terry are very happy.

_____

_____ 4. Kim wants a boy.

_____

_____ 5. The baby is due at the end of December.

_____

_____ 6. Terry is going to phone Kim.

_____

II. Word Review

Complete the sentences with these words.

so	**news**	**phone**	**great**

1. I should _____ my sister.

2–3. It's _____ hot today. It's a _____ day to go swimming.

4. Everyone knows about the fire. That's old _____.

due	**or**	**me too**	**beginning**

5. Do you live in a house _____ an apartment?

6. The teacher checks our homework at the _____ of class.

7. The telephone bill is _____ today.

8. Greg likes to play basketball. _____. It's my favorite sport.

A Better Job?

Listen to and pronounce these words.

Nouns	**Verbs**	**Other**
job	tell	better
post office	begin	glad

Complete the dialogue with these words and practice it with your partner.

post office	job	hear	begin	tell	better

Fran: I have something to _____ you.

Lynn: What is it?

Fran: I have a new _____.

Lynn: Is it _____ than the one you have?

Fran: Much.

Lynn: That's good news.

Fran: I _____ tomorrow.

Lynn: Where are you going to work?

Fran: In the _____.

Lynn: Will you make more money?

Fran: A lot more.

Lynn: I'm glad to _____ that.

Writing a Dialogue

Work with a partner and create your own dialogue. Use the words in this lesson and other words you know.

_____

A: I have something to tell you.

B: What is it?

A: I _____.

B: _____

A: _____

B: _____

A: _____

B: _____

Good and Bad News

Give three examples of good news.

1. _____
2. _____
3. _____

Give three examples of bad news.

1. _____
2. _____
3. _____

Months of the Year

December is the last month of the year. What are the first eleven months?

1. _____   5. _____   9. _____
2. _____   6. _____   10. _____
3. _____   7. _____   11. _____
4. _____   8. _____   12. December

Review

Reread the dialogue **Is She Pretty?** *(page 48 of* **The Pizza Tastes Great***) before doing the dialogue and word reviews.*

I. Dialogue Review

If the sentence is true, write **T.** *If it's false, write* **F** *and change it to a true statement.*

_____ 1. Today is Maria's birthday.

_____

_____ 2. Maria is Kathy's sister.

_____

_____ 3. Kathy is going to Maria's house after dinner.

_____

_____ 4. Maria is thirty years old.

_____

_____ 5. She's pretty and very nice.

_____

_____ 6. Steve is happy that she's married.

_____

II. Word Review

Complete the sentences with these words.

too   **cousins**   **birthday**   **age**

1. My _____ is July 9.

2. Alan plays the piano, and I do _____.

3. Doris doesn't want anyone to know her _____.

4. My mom and dad come from big families, and I have a lot of _____.

too bad   **married**   **how**   **pretty**

5. Eileen is _____. That's her husband.

6. I like your yard. It's very _____.

7. _____ tall is your brother?

8. It's _____ you can't go to the game tonight.

Is He Married?

Listen to and pronounce these words.

Verb	**Other**	
meet	older	handsome
	tonight	

Complete the dialogue with these words and practice it with your partner.

handsome   **older**   **meet**   **so**   **tonight**   **sure**

Tom: Today is my brother's birthday.

Ann: How old is he?

Tom: Ed's twenty-six.

Ann: Hmm. He's a little _____ than I am.

Tom: We're having a party for him _____.

Ann: Is Ed married?

Tom: No, he's single.

Ann: Is he _____?

Tom: I think _____.

Ann: Can I go to the party?

Tom: _____. Why not?

Ann: Thanks. I have to _____ him.

44

A Perfect _____

Write one paragraph of about seven or eight sentences describing the perfect girlfriend or boyfriend, or the perfect husband or wife. For example, "Donna is a perfect girlfriend. She . . ." "Jack is a perfect husband. He . . ."

_____

_____

_____

_____

_____

_____

_____

_____

How Important Is It?

Circle the number that tells how important it is (was) that the one you marry (married) a) be handsome or pretty; b) loves you a lot; etc.

1 = not important
2 = not that important
3 = important
4 = very important
5 = very, very important

A. be handsome or pretty	1	2	3	4	5
B. loves you a lot	1	2	3	4	5
C. understands you	1	2	3	4	5
D. has a lot of money	1	2	3	4	5
E. be intelligent	1	2	3	4	5
F. has a good education	1	2	3	4	5
G. likes what you like	1	2	3	4	5
H. be your age or close to it	1	2	3	4	5

Review

Reread the dialogue **A Cake** *(page 51 of* **The Pizza Tastes Great***) before doing the dialogue and word reviews.*

I. Dialogue Review

If the sentence is true, write **T.** *If it's false, write* **F** *and change it to a true statement.*

_____ 1. There are no bakeries near Leslie's house.

_____

_____ 2. Jackie wants to buy a birthday cake.

_____

_____ 3. It's his wife's birthday.

_____

_____ 4. Jackie is going to get some bread for Leslie.

_____

_____ 5. He's also getting some cookies for her.

_____

_____ 6. She's going to pay Jackie when he gets back.

_____

II. Word Review

Complete the sentences with these words.

near   **is there**   **bakery**   **anything**

1. _____ a doctor on the plane?

2. Mr. Rockefeller can buy _____ he wants.

3. Sit _____ the door.

4. I'm going to my favorite _____ to get some donuts.

pay   **whose**   **else**   **get**

5. _____ camera is on the table?

6. You can _____ by check.

7. What time do you _____ to school?

8. Who _____ is on the team?

Go Immediately

Listen to and pronounce these words.

Noun	**Verbs**	**Other**
hospital	drive	immediately
	should	ready

Complete the dialogue with these words and practice it with your partner.

ready   drive   terrible   hospital   should   pain

Chris: Is there a _____ near here?

Terry: Yes. I can _____ you there in two minutes.

Chris: Thanks.

Terry: What's the problem?

Chris: I have a _____ in my chest and arms.

Terry: Is it bad?

Chris: It's _____.

Terry: We _____ go immediately.

Chris: I'm _____.

Terry: Good. I'll get my car.

Chris: I hope it's not my heart.

Writing a Dialogue

Work with a partner and create your own dialogue. Use the words in this lesson and other words you know.

_____

A: Is there a _____ near here? (for example, bank, park, supermarket)

B: Yes, I can drive you there in two minutes.

A: Thanks.

B: _____

A: _____

B: _____

A: _____

B: _____

Why Are You Going to These Places?

Think of why you go to these places and complete the sentences.

1. I'm going to the supermarket to _____.

2. I'm going to the library to _____.

3. I'm going to the bank to _____.

4. I'm going to the pharmacy to _____.

5. I'm going to the park to _____.

6. I'm going to McDonald's to _____.

7. I'm going to the laundromat to _____.

8. I'm going to my friend's house to _____.

Review

Reread the dialogue **A Birthday Present** *(page 24 of* **The Pizza Tastes Great***) before doing the dialogue and word reviews.*

I. Dialogue Review

If the sentence is true, write **T.** *If it's false, write* **F** *and change it to a true statement.*

_____ 1. Jamie is going to get Ted a shirt for his birthday.

_____

_____ 2. She got him a sweater last year.

_____

_____ 3. She wants to get him something different this year.

_____

_____ 4. Chris asks about getting him a briefcase.

_____

_____ 5. Jamie likes that idea.

_____

_____ 6. Ted won't use the briefcase much.

_____

II. Word Review

Complete the sentences with these words.

of course   **briefcase**   **yet**   **got**

1. My husband isn't home _____.

2. Our teacher usually leaves his _____ on his desk.

3. Larry _____ his son a bicycle for Christmas.

4. _____ we'll help you.

how about   **let**   **different**   **one**

5. _____ me take your coat.

6. This store doesn't have what I want. I'm going to another _____.

7. _____ chicken soup for lunch?

8. We're moving our money to a _____ bank.

Married Twenty-Five Years

Listen to and pronounce these words.

Nouns		**Verbs**	**Other**
anniversary	camera	send	special
flower	picture	use	how long

Complete the dialogue with these words and practice it with your partner.

expensive   **special**   **send**   **how long**   **anniversary**   **camera**

Sandy: What can we get Bill and Sue for their _____?

Robin: I don't know. Let me think.

Sandy: We can _____ them flowers.

Robin: No, I don't want to do that.

Sandy: How about a _____?

Robin: That'll be _____.

Sandy: I know, but it's a _____ anniversary.

Robin: _____ will they be married?

Sandy: Twenty-five years.

Robin: Wow! That is special! Get the camera.

Sandy: They'll use it a lot.

Robin: Of course. They like to take pictures.

Interviewing

Ask your partner or some other person these questions.

1. May I ask you some questions?

2. When do people give presents?

3. Why do people give presents?

4. Name some presents that people often give.

5. Do you have a briefcase? Do you use it much?

6. Do you like to take pictures?

7. Do you take many?

8. When do people take pictures?

Sentence Completion

Complete these sentences.

1. I want to **get** a new _____.

2. I didn't _____ **yet**.

3. **Let** me_____.

4. **How about** _____?

5. My _____ is (are) **getting old**.

6. My _____ is (are) in my **briefcase**.

7. I _____ **every day**.

8. **Of course** I _____.

Of Course (Not)

Answer these questions with **Of course** *or* **Of course not;** *or* **Yes, I do** *or* **No, I don't.**

1. Do you want to be rich? _____

2. Do you like to get up early? _____

3. Do you like ice cream? _____

4. Do you want to learn English? _____

5. Do you speak Spanish? _____

6. Do you like the summer? _____

7. Do you watch TV at night? _____

Review

*Reread the story **Forty and Getting Gray** (page 56 of **The Pizza Tastes Great**) before doing the story, word, and word and story reviews.*

I. Story Review

If the sentence is true, write **T.** *If it's false, write* **F** *and change it to a true statement.*

_____ 1. Tom is relaxing and watching a movie.

_____

_____ 2. He makes a lot of money.

_____

_____ 3. Last year he saved a woman's life.

_____

_____ 4. He has a birthday next week.

_____

_____ 5. Tom's hair is getting gray, and he feels old.

_____

_____ 6. Gloria is sitting on the sofa and reading a book.

_____

_____ 7. She works for a large insurance company.

_____

_____ 8. She doesn't like her work.

_____

II. Word Review

Complete the sentences with these words.

every	**on fire**	**strong**	**relax**

1. Take a twenty-minute break and _____.

2. Oh no! Our house is _____!

3. Marina goes for a walk _____ afternoon.

4. You're _____. Help me carry these packages to the car.

feel	**pay attention**	**brave**	**last**

5. _____ to what you're doing.

6. Our _____ math test was long.

7. I don't _____ well. I'm not going to work.

8. The soldiers are fighting hard to save the city. They're _____.

III. Word and Story Review

A Firefighter

Complete the conversation with these words and practice it with your partner.

jog	computers	getting	insurance
well	saved	interesting	still

Pat: What's your job?

Tom: I'm a firefighter.

Pat: Do you like your work?

Tom: I love it. Last year I _____ a woman's life.

Pat: That's great!

Tom: Yes, and today's my birthday.

Pat: Happy birthday!

Tom: Thank you. I'm forty and my hair is _____ gray.

Pat: But you _____ look young.

Tom: Well, I play tennis every week, and I _____ a lot.

Pat: Are you married?

Tom: Yes. My wife works for a large _____ company.

Pat: That must be _____.

Tom: It is. She works with _____.

Pat: Does she like her job?

Tom: Yes, and it pays _____.

Pat: That's good.

Ben and Nancy

Read and enjoy the story about Ben and Nancy. Then write a similar story about a husband and wife.

It's nine o'clock at night, and Ben is watching a football game on TV. He loves football and watches it every Monday night during the football season. Ben is seventy-four and he's an engineer, but he doesn't work anymore. That's why he spends a lot of time watching TV, especially football games and old movies.

Ben's wife, Nancy, is sitting at the dining room table. She doesn't like football and never watches it on TV. Nancy is a high school English teacher, and she's correcting tests. Tomorrow is her birthday. She's going to be sixty-five, and her health is excellent. She never thinks of herself as old, but most of her students do. Of course they're only fifteen or sixteen, and they think a person is old at forty-five.

A Married Couple

After reading the story **Ben and Nancy,** *do one of the following.*

1. Write two paragraphs about a married couple. In the first paragraph, write about the husband. In the second paragraph, write about the wife.

2. Or write two paragraphs about any person or persons.

_____

_____

_____

_____

_____

_____

_____

_____

_____

_____

_____

_____

Review

Reread the story **On the Phone Too Much** *(page 60 of* **The Pizza Tastes Great***) before doing the story, word, and word and story reviews.*

I. Story Review

If the sentence is true, write **T.** *If it's false, write* **F** *and change it to a true statement.*

_____ 1. Dianne is twelve and in the seventh grade.

_____

_____ 2. She talks a lot on the phone.

_____

_____ 3. Tom or Gloria usually answers the phone.

_____

_____ 4. History and English are Dianne's favorite subjects.

_____

_____ 5. Dianne wants to study to be a chemist.

_____

_____ 6. Frank does all right in school.

_____

_____ 7. He likes to study.

_____

_____ 8. His big interests are basketball, music, and his girlfriend.

_____

II. Word Review

Complete the sentences with these words.

change	**magazine**	**answering**	**probably**

1. It'll _____ rain this afternoon.

2. Helen wants to _____ jobs. She doesn't like what she's doing.

3. The police are _____ a call for help.

4. This _____ has a lot of good pictures.

passed	**hope**	**inches**	**ringing**

5. I _____ Scott can come with us.

6. The alarm clock is _____. It's time to get up.

7. Michelle thinks she _____ the chemistry test.

8. The ruler is eighteen _____ long.

III. Word and Story Review

High School Students

Complete the conversation with these words and practice it with your partner.

best	usually	second	interests
subjects	hard	all right	favorites

Pat: How are Dianne and Frank?

Tom: Fine. Dianne is in her _____ year of high school.

Pat: Does she like school?

Tom: Yes, and she studies _____.

Pat: What _____ does she like?

Tom: Math and science are her _____.

Pat: Does she do well in them?

Tom: Yes, but we're having a problem. She's on the phone too much.

Pat: High school students _____ are.

Tom: I know, but we want her to change.

Pat: How's Frank doing in school?

Tom: _____, but he doesn't like to study.

Pat: What does he like to do?

Tom: His big _____ are basketball, music, and girls.

Pat: Is he a good basketball player?

Tom: He's the _____ player on the team.

Pat: That's wonderful!

Matching

In front of the words in column A, print the capital letters that are next to their definitions or descriptions in column B.

	Column A		Column B
_____	1. subjects	A.	to give money to
_____	2. get back	B.	up to now and now
_____	3. cousin	C.	math, science, history
_____	4. else	D.	to run
_____	5. pay	E.	what we use to carry important papers
_____	6. bakery	F.	to return
_____	7. usually	G.	more
_____	8. jog	H.	a store with cookies, cakes, and bread
_____	9. still	I.	a relative
_____	10. briefcase	J.	most of the time

Sentence Completion

Complete these sentences about yourself by writing **never, sometimes, often, usually**, *or* **always** *in the blank spaces.*

1. I _____ read the newspaper in the morning.

2. I _____ drink juice for breakfast.

3. I _____ chew gum.

4. I _____ listen to music.

5. I _____ go to the movies.

6. I _____ play cards.

7. I _____ watch the news on TV.

8. I _____ study at night.

4

Cars and Planes

Review

Reread the dialogue **Washing the Car** *(page 66 of* **The Pizza Tastes Great***) before doing the dialogue and word reviews.*

I. Dialogue Review

If the sentence is true, write **T.** *If it's false, write* **F** *and change it to a true statement.*

_____ 1. Don's in front of his house.

_____

_____ 2. He's fixing his car.

_____

_____ 3. His car is usually dirty.

_____

_____ 4. He takes good care of his car.

_____

_____ 5. He cleans his room a lot.

_____

_____ 6. His room is a mess.

_____

II. Word Review

Complete the sentences with these words.

mess	**always**	**in front of**	**in order**

1. There's an American flag _____ our school.

2. It was a big party, and our kitchen is a _____.

3. We don't have to clean this room. Everything is _____.

4. I _____ go to the bank on Friday afternoon.

right	**dirty**	**nothing**	**wash**

5–6. These windows are _____. I'm going to _____ them.

7. The doctor says I'll be fine. I hope he's _____.

8. If you want that box, take it. There's _____ in it.

That's What His Wife Says

Listen to and pronounce these words.

Noun	**Verbs**	**Other**
street	paint	across
	tell	right

Complete the dialogue with these words and practice it with your partner.

nice   **right**   **helping**   **tell**   **paint**   **across**

Fran: Where's Oscar?

Lynn: He's _____ the street.

Fran: What's he doing?

Lynn: He's _____ his friend.

Fran: To do what?

Lynn: To _____ his house.

Fran: That's _____ of Oscar.

Lynn: Yes, but don't _____ his wife.

Fran: Why not?

Lynn: He never does anything at home.

Fran: That's not _____.

Lynn: That's what his wife says.

60

Writing a Dialogue

Work with a partner and create your own dialogue. Use the words in this lesson and other words you know.

_____

A: Where's _____?

B: He's (She's) across the street.

A: What's he (she) doing?

B: _____

A: _____

B: _____

A: _____

B: _____

Sentence Completion

Complete these sentences about yourself by writing **never**, **sometimes**, **often**, **usually**, *or* **always** *in the blank spaces.*

1. I _____ clean my room.

2. I _____ keep things in order.

3. I _____ take good care of my clothes.

4. I _____ wash the dishes.

5. I _____ wash my clothes.

6. I _____ help keep the house clean.

7. I _____ brush my teeth after breakfast.

8. I _____ wash my hair at night.

Review

Reread the dialogue **Don't Worry** *(page 69 of* **The Pizza Tastes Great***) before doing the dialogue and word reviews.*

I. Dialogue Review

If the sentence is true, write **T.** *If it's false, write* **F** *and change it to a true statement.*

_____   1. Pat can't get into her car.

_____

_____   2. She doesn't know where her keys are.

_____

_____   3. The police officer doesn't want to help.

_____

_____   4. He can open the car with a coat hanger.

_____

_____   5. He goes to a store to get a hanger.

_____

_____   6. Pat thanks him.

_____

II. Word Review

Complete the sentences with these words.

> **trying**   **there's**   **hanger**   **officer**

1–2. I need a _____ for my jacket. _____ one in the closet.

3. Excuse me, _____. How do I get to the post office?

4. Alexi is _____ to learn English, but it's not easy.

> **kind**   **worry**   **waiting**   **thanks**

5–6. _____ for helping me with the dishes! It was very
_____ of you.

7. I'm _____ for the mail. It should be here by now.

8. Connie is rich. She never has to _____ about money.

I Can't Get into My House

Listen to and pronounce these words.

Nouns	**Verbs**	**Other**
ladder	forget	high
garage	climb	
	fall	

Complete the dialogue with these words and practice it with your partner.

climbing   fall   forget   high   maybe   garage

Dean: I can't get into my house.

Stacy: Did you _____ your keys?

Dean: Yes, they're in my house.

Stacy: _____ I can help.

Dean: How?

Stacy: By _____ in a window.

Dean: But the windows are _____.

Stacy: Do you have a ladder?

Dean: Yes, there's one in the _____.

Stacy: Good. Get it for me, please.

Dean: Here's the ladder. Be careful!

Stacy: Don't worry. I won't _____.

Interviewing

Ask your partner or some other person these questions.

1. May I ask you some questions?

2. Are you careful to lock your house or apartment when you go out?

3. Did you ever lock your house and then not have the key to get in?

4. Do you think it's a good idea to leave an extra key somewhere, or with someone, in case you don't have your key?

5. Do you think police officers are usually kind?

6. Do you think teachers are usually kind?

7. Do you worry a lot?

8. Name one thing you sometimes worry about.

Sentence Completion

Complete these sentences.

1. I never **worry** about _____.

2. I'm **trying** to _____.

3. I'm **kind** to _____.

4. It's **easy** to _____.

5. Sometimes I **forget** to _____.

6. **There's** a _____ in the kitchen.

Review

Reread the dialogue **A Car Loan** *(page 72 of* **The Pizza Tastes Great***) before doing the dialogue and word reviews.*

I. Dialogue Review

If the sentence is true, write **T.** *If it's false, write* **F** *and change it to a true statement.*

_____ 1. Sandy is going to take a bus to the bank.

_____

_____ 2. Lee has to cash a check.

_____

_____ 3. Sandy needs a loan.

_____

_____ 4. She's going to buy a house.

_____

_____ 5. Her car is five years old.

_____

_____ 6. New cars are very expensive.

_____

II. Word Review

Complete the sentences with these words.

apply	loan	wrong	costs

1. I don't need glasses. There's nothing _____ with my eyes.

2–4. Kristin is going to _____ for college soon. It

_____ a lot to go to college. That's why Kristin is going to ask the

bank for a _____.

about	cash	a lot of	have to

5. Where can I _____ this money order?

6. Mike gets home from work _____ six o'clock.

7. I _____ wash my hands before we eat.

8. When it's hot, I drink _____ water.

Buying a House

Listen to and pronounce these words.

Nouns		**Other**	
lawyer	block	wonderful	close
trouble	kid	far	away

Complete the dialogue with these words and practice it with your partner.

kids   trouble   close   far   lawyer   only

Omar: Where are you going?

Asma: I have to see a _____.

Omar: Are you in _____?

Asma: No, I'm going to buy a house.

Omar: That's wonderful. Is it _____ from here?

Asma: No, it's _____ four blocks away.

Omar: That's _____. I'm glad.

Asma: And it's only a block from the park.

Omar: That's nice for the _____.

Asma: That's right. They'll love it.

66

Writing a Dialogue

Work with a partner and create your own dialogue. Use the words in this lesson and other words you know.

_____

A: I'm going to buy a house.

B: That's wonderful. Is it far from here?

A: _____

B: _____

A: _____

B: _____

A: _____

B: _____

Sentence Completion

1. Tomorrow I **have to** _____.

2. Something is **wrong** with my _____.

3. I want to **buy** a _____.

4. It'll **cost** about _____.

5. I have **a lot of** _____.

6. I don't have **a lot of** _____.

7. I live **close** to _____.

8. I live **far** from _____.

9. People **apply** for loans and jobs. What else do people **apply** for? _____

_____.

Review

*Reread the dialogue **Afraid of Flying** (page 75 of **The Pizza Tastes Great**) before doing the dialogue and word reviews.*

I. Dialogue Review

*If the sentence is true, write **T**. If it's false, write **F** and change it to a true statement.*

_____ 1. Lynn is flying to Dallas, Texas.

_____

_____ 2. She's going there to visit a friend.

_____

_____ 3. Lynn and Terry like to fly.

_____

_____ 4. Lynn says flying is fast, comfortable, and safe.

_____

_____ 5. She thinks it's foolish to be afraid to fly.

_____

_____ 6. She says almost everyone feels safe in a plane.

_____

II. Word Review

Complete the sentences with these words.

afraid   **understand**   **safe**   **meeting**

1. It's not _____ to drink and drive.

2. Some students are _____ to ask questions.

3. What time is our _____?

4. Can you help me with these math problems? I don't _____ them.

foolish   **flying**   **maybe**   **comfortable**

5. The room has air conditioning. It'll be _____.

6. You're _____ to sit in the hot sun. It's not good for your skin.

7. The baby is crying. _____ he's hungry.

8. They're _____ the packages to Boston.

To Mexico

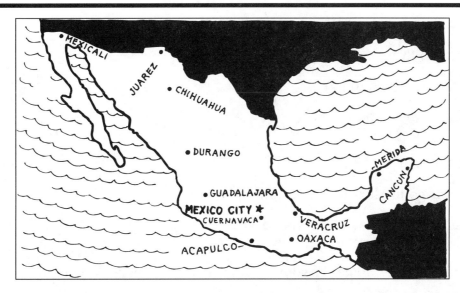

Listen to and pronounce these words.

Nouns	**Verbs**	**Other**
vacation	leave	excited
trip	pack	so = too = also

Complete the dialogue with these words and practice it with your partner.

excited   second   yet   trip   leaving   so

Chris: Where are you going for your vacation?

Jackie: To Mexico.

Chris: Is this your first time?

Jackie: No, it's our _____.

Chris: When are you _____?

Jackie: Tomorrow morning at eight.

Chris: Did you pack?

Jackie: Not _____.

Chris: You must be _____.

Jackie: Yes. And _____ are the kids.

Chris: Have a nice _____!

Jackie: Thanks. We will.

Interviewing

Ask your partner or some other person these questions.

1. May I ask you some questions?

2. Do you like to fly?

3. Do you think it's safe to fly?

4. What do you know about Texas?

5. Where is Mexico?

6. Did you ever go to Mexico? If you did, why?

7. What language do most Mexicans speak?

8. Do you usually stay home for your vacation? If not, where do you go?

Sentence Completion

Complete these sentences.

1. I don't **understand** _____.

2. I think it's **foolish** to _____.

3. It's **safe** to _____.

4. It's not **safe** to _____.

5. I'm **afraid** of (to) _____.

6. I'm not **afraid** of (to) _____.

Review

Reread the story **Two Boyfriends** *(page 78 of* **The Pizza Tastes Great***) before doing the story, word, and word and story reviews.*

I. Story Review

If the sentence is true, write **T.** *If it's false, write* **F** *and change it to a true statement.*

_____ 1. Linda is a good secretary.

_____

_____ 2. She types fast, but she makes a lot of mistakes.

_____

_____ 3. She's pretty and likes to dance.

_____

_____ 4. Mike is her only boyfriend.

_____

_____ 5. Mike and Linda go to the movies every Saturday night.

_____

_____ 6. Mike and Ray are friends.

_____

_____ 7. Linda likes Mike a lot, but she doesn't want to marry him.

_____

_____ 8. She knows she's going to hurt Mike's feelings.

_____

II. Word Review

Complete the sentences with these words.

lawyer   **mistake**   **hurts**   **either**

1. Matt drank too much beer at the party. It was a _____.
2. You have to study hard to be a _____.
3. I don't play cards, and my wife doesn't _____.
4. Allyson can't play tennis today. Her foot _____.

answer   **mechanic**   **truth**   **fair**

5. Tell me what happened. I have to know the _____.
6. Your father is calling you. _____ him!
7. Regina and I do the same work and get the same pay. That's _____.
8. The _____ says it'll cost seven hundred dollars to fix our car.

III. Word and Story Review

A New Disco

Complete the conversation with these words and practice it with your partner.

excellent	busy	filing	also
fixed	fun	soon	however

Linda: Good afternoon. Mr. Clark's office.

Mike: Hi, Linda. Are you _____?

Linda: Very. _____, for you, I have time.

Mike: What are you doing?

Linda: _____ some letters.

Mike: I want to take you to a new disco Saturday night.

Linda: Great, that sounds like _____.

Mike: Yeah, the music is _____.

Linda: Did you check my car yet?

Mike: Yes, and I _____ the brakes.

Linda: Good. Any other problems?

Mike: You're _____ going to need new tires.

Linda: When?

Mike: Not now, but _____.

Linda: Thanks for your help!

Mike: It's nothing. See you Saturday night.

In Love

Read and enjoy the story about Joyce and Wayne. Then write a similar story about a young couple in love.

Joyce is a nurse at a busy hospital. It's not an easy job, but she loves it. She likes to help people and is very understanding. She's always pleasant and kind to the patients, and that helps them a lot. Joyce is single and twenty-five. But she's not going to be single very long. She's in love with a young doctor who works with her at the hospital. His name is Wayne.

Wayne is twenty-eight. He isn't handsome, but he's very smart and an excellent doctor. He works long hours and doesn't have much time to spend with Joyce. But he loves her very much and takes her out to dinner when he has a day off. They plan to get married in May and fly to Puerto Rico for their honeymoon.

A Young Couple

After reading the story **In Love,** *do one of the following.*

1. Write two paragraphs about a young couple who are single and in love. In the first paragraph, write about the young woman, and in the second, about the young man.

2. Or write two paragraphs about any person or persons.

_____

_____

_____

_____

_____

_____

_____

_____

_____

_____

_____

_____

_____

_____

_____

Review

Reread the story **Will Linda Say Yes?** *(page 81 of* **The Pizza Tastes Great***) before doing the story, word, and word and story reviews.*

I. Story Review

If the sentence is true, write **T.** *If it's false, write* **F** *and change it to a true statement.*

_____   1. Ray's pay is low.

_____

_____   2. Heavy traffic and wild drivers make his job difficult.

_____

_____   3. He's big and likes to eat.

_____

_____   4. On Sunday, Linda cooks dinner for him.

_____

_____   5. After dinner, Ray and Linda like to go for a walk.

_____

_____   6. When the weather is bad, they watch TV.

_____

_____   7. Linda loves and understands Ray.

_____

_____   8. He's rich and handsome.

_____

II. Word Review

Complete the sentences with these words.

salary   **wind**   **future**   **wild**

1. The _____ flowers are pretty.

2. My _____ is going up next month. I'm very happy.

3. I don't worry about the past. I think about the _____

4. The _____ is coming from the south. That's why it's so hot.

| usually | handsome | hope | nervous |

5. Ken isn't _____, but he's very nice.

6. Lucy is _____. She's going to the dentist.

7. I _____ read the newspaper before I go to work.

8. Our team isn't playing well, but the game isn't over. There's still _____.

III. Word and Story Review

A Big Question

Complete the conversation with these words and practice it with your partner.

| appetite | eat out | passengers | of course |
| traffic | polite | difficult | heavy |

Linda: This is my favorite restaurant. I love to _____.

Ray: Me too! You know what a (an) _____ I have.

Linda: How was your day?

Ray: Long and _____.

Linda: Was there a lot of _____?

Ray: No. It wasn't that _____.

Linda: Were the _____ the problem?

Ray: Yes, most were _____, but some were terrible.

Linda: Forget about them and enjoy your dinner.

Ray: I will, but first I have a big question for you.

Linda: What is it?

Ray: Do you love me a lot?

Linda: Yes, I'm crazy about you.

Ray: Will you marry me?

Linda: _____ I will!

Ray: I hope you like this.

Linda: What a beautiful ring! Thank you!

Matching

In front of the words in column A, print the capital letters that are next to their definitions or descriptions in column B.

	Column A	Column B
_____	1. mess	A. to ask for in writing
_____	2. worry	B. money you must pay back
_____	3. get in	C. what birds do
_____	4. apply	D. desire to eat
_____	5. file	E. to be nervous
_____	6. fly	F. a person who fixes cars
_____	7. comfortable	G. no order
_____	8. loan	H. how much money you make
_____	9. mechanic	I. to put papers in a cabinet
_____	10. salary	J. a person who travels on a bus, train, or plane
_____	11. appetite	K. to enter
_____	12. passenger	L. what you want a chair to be

Talking It Over

Discuss these questions with another student or in a small group.

1. Do you think it's fair for a single girl to have two boyfriends? Explain your answer.

2. Linda has a lot of fun dancing with Mike. Complete this sentence. I think it's fun to _____.

3. How much education does a secretary need?

4. How much money do you think a secretary makes in a year? A mechanic? A bus driver? A nurse?

5. What do you think is a good salary?

6. How important is money to you? (a) very important (b) important (c) not that important

7. What do you hope to be or do in the future?

5

Work and Shopping

Review

Reread the dialogue **On Sale** *(page 87 of* **The Pizza Tastes Great***) before doing the dialogue and word reviews.*

I. Dialogue Review

If the sentence is true, write **T**. *If it's false, write* **F** *and change it to a true statement.*

_____   1. Lee is wearing a new coat.

_____

_____   2. Fran doesn't like it.

_____

_____   3. It was very expensive.

_____

_____   4. It was on sale.

_____

_____   5. Lee got it at a small store.

_____

_____   6. Fran likes to shop at Sears.

_____

II. Word Review

Complete the sentences with these words.

how much	shop	price	looks
terrific	on sale	too	glad

1. Paul _____ terrible. Is he sick?

2. Debbie likes country music, and I do _____.

3–4. Mrs. Barsky is a _____ teacher. My son is _____ he has her.

5. _____ was your new bike?

6. The _____ of vegetables goes up in the winter.

7. I'm going to buy these shoes. They look okay and they're _____.

8. When do you usually _____?

Missing Lines

Use the following lines to complete the miniconversations.

Where do you like to shop?   Where did you get that book?
Tomorrow morning.   How much was your VCR?
You look terrific.

1. **Pat:** When does the sale begin?

   Lee: _____

2. **Pat:** _____

   Lee: From the library.

3. **Pat:** _____

   Lee: Thank you.

4. **Pat:** _____

   Lee: In the department stores at the mall.

5. **Pat:** _____

   Lee: Three hundred dollars.

A New Car

79

Listen to and pronounce these words.

Noun	**Verb**	**Other**
power	's got = has got	cheap

Complete the dialogue with these words and practice it with your partner.

careful   **cheap**   **power**   **worry**   **drive**   **cost**

Sandy: Do you like my new car?

Terry: Yeah, it looks great.

Sandy: And it's got a lot of _____.

Terry: Can I _____ it?

Sandy: Okay, but be _____!

Terry: I will. Don't _____.

Sandy: Here are the keys. Get in.

Terry: Thanks. How much did the car _____?

Sandy: Eighteen thousand.

Terry: That's not bad.

Sandy: No, it isn't. New cars aren't _____.

Writing a Dialogue

Work with a partner and create your own dialogue. Use the words in this lesson and any words you know.

_____

A: Do you like my new _____?

B: Yeah, it looks _____.

A: _____

B: _____

A: _____

B: _____

A: _____

B: _____

About How Much?

About how much do you think these things cost? The clothing is good, and it's on sale at Sears. (If possible, one of the students should bring to class an ad from Sears or another department store so the class can check the prices after they do this exercise.)

1. A pair of sneakers costs about _____.

2. A dress costs about _____.

3. A man's suit costs about _____.

4. A pair of jeans costs about _____.

5. A man's belt costs about _____.

6. A blouse costs about _____.

7. A skirt costs about _____.

8. A shirt costs about _____.

9. A tie costs about _____.

10. A new small car—for example, a Ford Escort—costs about _____.

Review

Reread the dialogue **A New Dress** *(page 90 of* **The Pizza Tastes Great***) before doing the dialogue and word reviews.*

I. Dialogue Review

If the sentence is true, write **T.** *If it's false, write* **F** *and change it to a true statement.*

_____   1. Janet's key is in her handbag.

_____

_____   2. Kevin lets her in.

_____

_____   3. Janet got a new dress.

_____

_____   4. Kevin is happy his wife got a new dress.

_____

_____   5. Janet doesn't have a lot of dresses.

_____

_____   6. The dresses she has aren't in style.

_____

II. Word Review

Complete the sentences with these words.

in style	**let**	**one**	**full of**
get	**wrong**	**other**	**honey**

1. This TV is okay, but I'm going to buy a better _____.

2. Shawn is going to the bakery to _____ some rolls and cookies.

3. _____ me know what time the party begins.

4. Jessica's math teacher isn't very good, but her _____ teachers are excellent.

5. The baby has a box _____ toys.

6. Ted's in the hospital, but we don't know what's _____ with him.

7. Can I help you paint the kitchen, _____?

8. Short hair is _____, but Nancy and I don't like it.

An Hour Late

Listen to and pronounce these words.

Noun
midnight

Verbs
won't = will not
mean

Other
around = about

Complete the dialogue with these words and practice it with your partner.

around   **won't**   **safe**   **tell**   **sorry**   **means**

Mother: Is that you, Diego?

Diego: Yes, it is.

Mother: Come in. Thank God you're _____!

Diego: I'm _____ that I'm a little late.

Mother: A little late? Do you know what time it is?

Diego: _____ twelve-thirty.

Mother: It's one o'clock.

Diego: What time did you _____ me to be home?

Mother: By midnight.

Diego: That _____ I'm only an hour late.

Mother: An hour is a long time to wait.

Diego: You're right. I _____ be late again.

Interviewing

Ask your partner or some other person these questions.

1. May I ask you some questions?

2. Do you like to shop?

3. Do you have a favorite store where you shop? What's its name?

4. Can a person save a lot of money by buying clothes when they're on sale?

5. Do you spend a lot of money on clothes?

6. How important is it to be "in style"? (a) very important (b) important (c) not that important

7. What color clothes do you like best?

8. When you buy clothes, are you fast or are you slow and careful?

What Do You Wear?

Complete these sentences.

1. I like to wear _____.

2. I don't like to wear _____.

3. When it's very cold, I wear _____.

4. When it's hot, I wear _____.

5. When I want to relax, I wear _____.

6. When I go to school (work), I usually wear _____.

Review

Reread the dialogue **A Cashier** *(page 93 of* **The Pizza Tastes Great***) before doing the dialogue and word reviews.*

I. Dialogue Review

If the sentence is true, write **T.** *If it's false, write* **F** *and change it to a true statement.*

_____   1. Chris is a cashier at Sears.

_____

_____   2. He doesn't like his job.

_____

_____   3. He makes a lot of money.

_____

_____   4. He's looking for another job.

_____

_____   5. It's easy to find one.

_____

_____   6. Gerry tells him to keep looking and he'll get one.

_____

II. Word Review

Complete the sentences with these words.

interesting	**kinds**	**should**	**keep**
looking for	**another**	**find**	**little**

1. Letter carriers work in all _____ of weather.

2. Dinner is going to be a _____ late tonight.

3. Nicole is _____ her pen.

4. _____ studying, and you'll do well in the exam.

5. May I have _____ slice of pizza?

6. We _____ pay these bills.

7. Newsweek is a very _____ magazine.

8. I can't _____ my gloves. Did you see them?

Missing Lines

Use the following lines to complete the miniconversations.

Are you looking for another job?   Why is Regina so thin?
That won't be easy to find.   He's very nice.
Of course, he's a mechanic.

1. **Jackie:** What kind of person is Mr. Daniels?

   Leslie: _____

2. **Jackie:** _____

   Leslie: No, I like what I'm doing.

3. **Jackie:** Is Billy good at fixing cars?

   Leslie: _____

4. **Jackie:** _____

   Leslie: She eats very little.

5. **Jackie:** We're looking for a nice house that doesn't cost a lot.

   Leslie: _____

A Carpenter

Listen to and pronounce these words.

Nouns		**Verb**
carpenter	company	build
construction	ad	

Complete the dialogue with these words and practice it with your partner.

there's   build   company   fix   ad   construction

Robin: What kind of work do you do?

Stacy: I'm a carpenter. I work for a _____ company.

Robin: Do you _____ new houses?

Stacy: No, we _____ old ones.

Robin: Do you like your work?

Stacy: Sure. But _____ one problem.

Robin: What's that?

Stacy: Sometimes the _____ doesn't have any work.

Robin: What do you do then?

Stacy: I put a (an) _____ in the newspaper.

Robin: Good idea. People always need carpenters.

Writing a Dialogue

Work with a partner and create your own dialogue. Use the words in this lesson and other words you know.

_____

A: What kind of work do you do?

B: I'm a (an) _____.

A: Do you like what you're doing?

B: _____

A: _____

B: _____

A: _____

B: _____

How Interesting Are These Jobs?

Read the list of ten jobs. Then circle how interesting each job would be for **you.**

1 = not interesting

2 = not that interesting

3 = interesting

4 = very interesting

5 = very, very interesting

A. secretary	1	2	3	4	5
B. teacher	1	2	3	4	5
C. nurse	1	2	3	4	5
D. lawyer	1	2	3	4	5
E. computer programmer	1	2	3	4	5
F. carpenter	1	2	3	4	5
G. auto mechanic	1	2	3	4	5
H. salesperson	1	2	3	4	5
I. store manager	1	2	3	4	5
J. businessman/businesswoman	1	2	3	4	5

Review

Reread the dialogue **I Hate to Get Up** *(page 96 of* **The Pizza Tastes Great***) before doing the dialogue and word reviews.*

I. Dialogue Review

If the sentence is true, write **T.** *If it's false, write* **F** *and change it to a true statement.*

_____   1. Pat doesn't like to get up in the morning.

   _____

_____   2. She gets up at six-thirty.

   _____

_____   3. She has to be at work by seven.

   _____

_____   4. Pat thinks Carol is lucky.

   _____

_____   5. Carol owns a clothing store.

   _____

_____   6. Carol's store opens at ten.

   _____

II. Word Review

Complete the sentences with these words.

have to	**me too**	**lucky**	**hate**
until	**get up**	**early**	**own**

1. I'm hot. _____. I'm going to open a window.

2–3. Mr. and Mrs. Meyer _____ two large houses and an expensive boat. They _____ be rich.

4. If you don't _____ now, you'll be late for work.

5. Megan was in a bad accident. She's _____ to be alive.

6. Eric can't go out and play _____ he does his homework.

7. Most people like onions, but I _____ them.

8. I don't feel well. I want to go home _____.

I Work Nights

Listen to and pronounce these words.

Nouns		**Verb**	**Other**
security	parking lot	check	lazy
airport			really

Complete the dialogue with these words and practice it with your partner.

until   lots   lazy   security   spend   really

Fran: I hate to get up in the morning.

Lynn: That's a problem I don't have. I sleep all morning.

Fran: You must be _____.

Lynn: Not _____. I work nights.

Fran: What hours do you work?

Lynn: From eleven P.M. _____ seven A.M.

Fran: And what do you do?

Lynn: I work for _____ at Newark Airport.

Fran: Is your job interesting?

Lynn: Not very.

Fran: Why not?

Lynn: I _____ most of my time checking the parking _____.

Interviewing

Ask your partner or some other person these questions.

1. May I ask you some questions?

2. How many hours do you usually sleep?

3. Do you think you should get more sleep than that?

4. What time do you have to be at work (school)?

5. What time do you finish work (school)?

6. When do you work best? In the morning? In the afternoon? At night?

7. What's good about having your own business?

8. Do you want to have your own business?

Sentence Completion

Complete these sentences.

1. I'm **lucky** because I _____.

2. I don't **own** a _____, but some day I hope to have one.

3. I have my **own** _____.

4. I **spend** a lot of time _____.

5. I **hate** to _____.

6. Are you **lazy**? _____. Explain your answer. _____.

Review

Reread the story **A Busy Shoe Store** *(page 99 of* **The Pizza Tastes Great***) before doing the story, word, and word and story reviews.*

I. Story Review

If the sentence is true, write **T.** *If it's false, write* **F** *and change it to a true statement.*

_____   1. Eddie is in the second grade.

_____

_____   2. He takes swimming lessons every week.

_____

_____   3. Mary is a good student and wants to be a lawyer.

_____

_____   4. Paul and Rita own a store that sells men's shoes.

_____

_____   5. Paul works hard, but Rita is lazy.

_____

_____   6. Their store opens at ten A.M. and usually closes at six P.M.

_____

_____   7. Paul or Rita is always in the store.

_____

_____   8. Paul is good at working with the children and their parents.

_____

II. Word Review

Complete the sentences with these words.

stay	**or**	**beginning**	**both**
almost	**close**	**together**	**order**

1–2. It's _____ to rain. Tell the children to _____ in the house and play.

3. Sharon and I are going to study _____ for our science test.

4. Do you want to watch TV _____ go for a walk?

5. Abdul is _____ six feet tall.

6. The teachers _____ the books for their classes.

7. What time does the post office _____?

8. We're _____ hungry. We should stop and eat.

III. Word and Story Review

Getting Big

Jack and Rita are old friends.

Complete the conversation with these words and practice it with your partner.

already	learning	run	count
lessons	especially	next	sell

Jack: How old is Eddie?

Rita: He's almost four.

Jack: He must be getting big.

Rita: Yes. He's taking swimming _____ and going to nursery school.

Jack: What's he _____ at the nursery?

Rita: The alphabet and how to _____.

Jack: That's great. And how old is Mary?

Rita: Thirteen. She'll be in high school _____ year.

Jack: I can't believe she's thirteen _____.

Rita: Yes, and she wants to be a lawyer.

Jack: That's nice. Do you and Rita still _____ the shoe store?

Rita: Yes, we still _____ shoes.

Jack: How's business?

Rita: Fine. We're very busy, _____ on Saturdays.

A Small Grocery Store

Read and enjoy the story about Anna and Bogdan. Then write a similar story.

Anna and Bogdan are married and have two children, Marina and Jan. They're from Poland, and they own and run a small grocery store. It's not an easy job. The store opens at six in the morning and closes at eight at night. Either Anna or Bogdan is usually in the store. Their prices are higher than in a supermarket, but people go to their store because it's closer to home. Most people buy only a few things, for example, milk and bread. The store is doing well, but the hours are long.

Marina is nineteen, and she's in her first year in college. She lives at home and goes to a state college. She likes to study, is very smart, and wants to be a dentist.

Jan is thirteen and is in the eighth grade. He's also a good student, but what Jan really likes are sports. He's a good swimmer and a great basketball player. He plays basketball for his school team.

A Family

Write a story similar to **A Small Grocery Store,** *or write a story about any person or persons.*

_____

_____

_____

_____

_____

_____

_____

_____

_____

_____

_____

_____

_____

_____

_____

_____

_____

Review

Reread the story **Quiet and Very Serious** *(page 102 of* **The Pizza Tastes Great***) before doing the story, word, and word and story reviews.*

I. Story Review

If the sentence is true, write **T.** *If it's false, write* **F** *and change it to a true statement.*

_____　1. Paul gets angry quickly and is very serious.

　　　_____

_____　2. He has a lot of friends.

　　　_____

_____　3. Rita likes to talk and tell jokes.

　　　_____

_____　4. She gets angry a lot.

　　　_____

_____　5. Paul and Rita often fight about the children.

　　　_____

_____　6. He shouts at the children and hits them.

　　　_____

_____　7. Rita lets the children do anything they want.

　　　_____

_____　8. She's kind and patient.

　　　_____

II. Word Review

Complete the sentences with these words.

laughing	**quickly**	**angry**	**smiles**
shout	**joke**	**however**	**kidding**

1. Amy looks so pretty when she _____.

2. I hope you're not _____ at my hat.

3. Jeff drives fast. _____, he's never had an accident.

4. There's no need to _____. Talk quietly.

5. Time goes _____ when you're busy.

6. Denise says her father knows the president, but I'm sure she's _____.

7. Vince is _____ at me. That's why he's not coming to my party.

8. Do you want to hear a good _____? I think you'll like it.

III. Word and Story Review

Too Strict

Complete the conversation with these words and practice it with your partner.

fighting	afraid	true	correcting
forget	completely	hit	obey

Rita: You're too strict with the children.

Paul: Why do you say that?

Rita: Because you're always _____ them.

Paul: Maybe, but do I ever _____ them?

Rita: No, but they're _____ of you.

Paul: So what? That's good!

Rita: No, it isn't. You _____ they're only children.

Paul: No, I don't. The problem is you're too easy on them.

Rita: That's not _____.

Paul: Yes, it is. You let them do anything they want.

Rita: No, I don't. They always listen to and _____ me.

Paul: Why are we _____ about the children again?

Rita: Because we're _____ different.

Paul: How did we ever get married?

Rita: I don't know. That's a good question.

Matching

In front of the words in column A, print the capital letters that are next to their definitions or descriptions in column B.

	Column A	**Column B**
_____	1. Sears	A. place to keep clothes
_____	2. full	B. not talking
_____	3. on sale	C. to joke
_____	4. closet	D. large department store
_____	5. supermarket	E. to do what someone tells you
_____	6. kid (verb)	F. no more space
_____	7. obey	G. where we buy food
_____	8. correct	H. it's easy to hear people when they do this
_____	9. quiet	I. low price
_____	10. shout	J. to tell someone they're wrong

What's Your Opinion?

Give your opinion of each of these statements by circling **A, B, or C.**

A = true

B = not true

C = I don't know

1. It's important for children to learn to swim.	A	B	C
2. It's important for children to go to nursery school.	A	B	C
3. Most children watch too much TV.	A	B	C
4. It's difficult for a husband and a wife to run a business together.	A	B	C
5. Most wives talk more than their husbands.	A	B	C
6. It's difficult to be a good parent.	A	B	C
7. Parents should not shout at their children.	A	B	C
8. Many parents are too easy with their children.	A	B	C

6

The Weather

Review

*Reread the dialogue **A Hot Day** (page 108 of **The Pizza Tastes Great**) before doing the dialogue and word reviews.*

I. Dialogue Review

*If the sentence is true, write **T**. If it's false, write **F** and change it to a true statement.*

_____ 1. Terry and Gene like the heat.

_____

_____ 2. Terry wants a cold drink.

_____

_____ 3. Gene hates to work in hot weather.

_____

_____ 4. The hot weather makes Terry lazy.

_____

_____ 5. And it makes it easy for Gene to sleep.

_____

_____ 6. It'll be hotter next week.

_____

II. Word Review

Complete the sentences with these words.

lazy	tastes	weather	hates
must	would	cooler	killing

1. I don't want to go for a walk. My feet are _____ me.

2. _____ you like to dance?

3. There's nothing we can do about the _____.

4. Valerie isn't going to school today. She _____ be sick.

5. Hakeem _____ to shop.

6. The soup _____ terrible. There's too much salt in it.

7. The children are playing in the basement. It's _____ there.

8. Ralph eats a lot, sleeps a lot, and watches a lot of TV, but he doesn't do much. He's _____.

Missing Lines

Use the following lines to complete the miniconversations.

Why are you watching TV so late?
Do you want something to drink?
Next week.

Please. It tastes good.
Do I need a jacket?

1. **Sandy:** _____

   Chris: Yes, it's getting cooler.

2. **Sandy:** When's Carlos going to Mexico?

   Chris: _____

3. **Sandy:** _____

   Chris: I can't sleep.

4. **Sandy:** Would you like some more turkey?

   Chris: _____

5. **Sandy:** _____

   Chris: No thanks. I'm not thirsty.

Cold Weather

Listen to and pronounce these words.

Nouns	**Verbs**	**Other**	
wonder	turn up	out	clear
report	put on	warm	

Complete the dialogue with these words and practice it with your partner.

report   **out**   **turn up**   **clear**   **put on**   **wonder**

Fran: I hate this cold weather.

Pat: Me too! It's only twenty degrees _____.

Fran: And it's not very warm in the house.

Pat: Let me check the temperature.

Fran: What is it?

Pat: Sixty-two degrees.

Fran: No _____ I'm cold!

Pat: Why don't you _____ a sweater?

Fran: Good idea.

Pat: And I'll _____ the heat.

Fran: Thanks.

Pat: What's the weather _____ for tomorrow?

Fran: _____ and colder.

Pat: Oh no! I'm moving to Florida.

Writing a Dialogue

Work with a partner and create your own dialogue. Use the words in this lesson and other words you know.

_____

A: I hate this _____ weather. (cold, hot, rainy)

B: Me too! _____

A: _____

B: _____

A: _____

B: _____

A: _____

B: _____

Word Building

*Add **y** to these nouns to make them adjectives. Drop the **e** in **ice*** and double the **n** in **sun*** before adding **y**.*

Noun	Adjective	Meaning
rain	_____	lots of rain
snow	_____	lots of snow
*ice	_____	lots of ice
*sun	_____	lots of sun
cloud	_____	lots of clouds
wind	_____	lots of wind

Sentence Completion

Complete these sentences.

1. When it's **sunny**, I like to _____.

2. When it's **rainy**, I like to _____.

3. It must be about _____ **degrees** now.

4. I **would like** a (to) _____.

5. _____ **taste(s)** good.

6. **Next** week I _____.

Review

Reread the dialogue **Not a Cloud in the Sky** *(page 111 of* **The Pizza Tastes Great***) before doing the dialogue and word reviews.*

I. Dialogue Review

If the sentence is true, write **T**. *If it's false, write* **F** *and change it to a true statement.*

_____ 1. There are some clouds in the sky.

_____

_____ 2. Jackie asks what the temperature is.

_____

_____ 3. Jackie loves October, but Robin doesn't.

_____

_____ 4. Fall is the season Jackie and Robin like the most.

_____

_____ 5. The weather isn't very good in the fall.

_____

_____ 6. The leaves are beautiful in the fall.

_____

II. Word Review

Complete the sentences with these words.

temperature	favorite	there's	season
leaves	mine	degrees	change

1. _____ a phone in the kitchen.

2. The teacher is going to _____ my seat. I talk too much.

3. Is that your umbrella or _____?

4. The _____ is only twenty-six. You'll need a warm coat.

5. In most schools, the basketball _____ begins in December and ends in March.

6. It's going to be a hot day. It's eighty-five _____ already.

7. After dinner, I sit in my _____ chair and read the newspaper or watch TV.

8. There are no _____ on the trees in winter.

I Love Spring

Listen to and pronounce these words.

Nouns		**Verbs**	**Other**
bird	grass	shine	icy
road	air	sing	fresh

Complete the dialogue with these words and practice it with your partner.

birds **look** **icy** **shining** **fresh** **grass**

Kim Young: What a great day!

Ho Sook: It sure is. The sun is _____.

Kim Young: The _____ are singing.

Ho Sook: And there'll be no more snow.

Kim Young: Or _____ roads.

Ho Sook: The _____ will be green soon.

Kim Young: And the flowers will _____ so pretty.

Ho Sook: Are the kids outside?

Kim Young: Yes, they're playing baseball in the park.

Ho Sook: Good. They need the _____ air.

Kim Young: I love spring.

Ho Sook: So do I. It's my favorite season.

104

Interviewing

Ask your partner or some other person these questions.

1. May I ask you some questions?

2. Do you often watch the weather report on TV? Do you often listen to it on the radio?

3. Describe today's weather.

4. What do you like to do in the summer?

5. Do you spend much time in the sun?

6. In the summer many people use sun lotion to protect their skin from the sun? Do you?

7. What do you like to eat in the summer?

8. Do you eat more in the summer, or less?

What Do You Think?

What temperature do you consider very cold, cold, cool, warm, hot, very hot? Use the Fahrenheit scale. (Fahrenheit is the temperature scale generally used in the United States.)

1. very cold = _____

2. cold = _____

3. cool = _____

4. warm = _____

5. hot = _____

6. very hot = _____

Sports

Many sports have a special season or seasons. List the season when we usually play each sport. Some sports may have more than one season.

1. baseball   _____

2. football   _____

3. basketball (indoors)   _____

4. soccer (outdoors)   _____

5. swimming (outdoors)   _____

6. golf   _____

7. tennis (outdoors)   _____

8. skiing   _____

Review

Reread the dialogue **Cold and Windy** *(page 114 of* **The Pizza Tastes Great***) before doing the dialogue and word reviews.*

I. Dialogue Review

If the sentence is true, write **T***. If it's false, write* **F** *and change it to a true statement.*

_____ 1. It's cold, but there's little wind.

_____

_____ 2. Carol is going to wear her heavy coat.

_____

_____ 3. She's going to the bank.

_____

_____ 4. She's going to mail a package.

_____

_____ 5. Lynn wants ten stamps.

_____

_____ 6. Carol will return in about an hour.

_____

II. Word Review

Complete the sentences with these words.

buy	heavy	wears	windy
out	be back	mail	would

1. The Sunday newspapers are very _____.

2–3. Is it snowing _____? Yes, and it's very _____. That's why it feels so cold.

4. Our sofa is getting old. We should _____ a new one.

5. I have a birthday card for Mario. I'm going to _____ it today.

6. _____ you answer the phone, please?

7. Ms. Barton usually _____ a suit to work.

8. I have to go to Chicago, but I'll _____ tomorrow.

Missing Lines

Use the following lines to complete the miniconversations.

How many donuts do you want?   I'm sorry, but I can't now. I'm very busy.
What are you going to wear to school? To visit his sister. She's sick.
Donna is in Los Angeles on business.

1. **Jan:** _____

   Gale: Blue jeans and a sweater.

2. **Jan:** Where is Fred going?

   Gale: _____

3. **Jan**: _____

   Gale: Give me six, please.

4. **Jan:** _____

   Gale: Do you know when she'll be back?

5. **Jan:** Would you help me clean the garage?

   Gale: _____

Jogging

Listen to and pronounce these words.

Nouns	**Verb**	**Other**
exercise	jog	twice
nap		better

Complete the dialogue with these words and practice it with your partner.

> **fun**   **nap**   **jog**   **better**   **twice**   **should**

Tracy: Is it windy out?

Kelly: No, not now. Where are you going?

Tracy: To the park to _____.

Kelly: Do you jog every day?

Tracy: No, _____ a week.

Kelly: Is it _____?

Tracy: Not really, but it makes me feel _____.

Kelly: I don't get any exercise.

Tracy: You _____. Do you want to come with me?

Kelly: No. I'm going to watch TV and take a _____.

Tracy: I think you're lazy.

Kelly: Very.

Writing a Dialogue

Work with a partner and create your own dialogue. Use the words in this lesson and other words you know.

_____

A: Where are you going?

B: To the park to _____.

A: Do you _____ in the park often?

B: _____

A: _____

B: _____

A: _____

B: _____

The Post Office

Answer these questions about the post office.

1. List five different reasons why people go to the post office.

   A. _____

   B. _____

   C. _____

   D. _____

   E. _____

2. Is working in the post office a good job? Explain your answer.

3. Do you think the U.S. post office does a good job? Explain your answer.

4. How much does it cost to send a letter in the United States?

5. What's your zip code?

Review

Reread the dialogue **It's Beginning to Snow** *(page 117 of* **The Pizza Tastes Great***) before doing the dialogue and word reviews.*

I. Dialogue Review

If the sentence is true, write **T**. *If it's false, write* **F** *and change it to a true statement.*

_____ 1. Lee likes snow.

_____

_____ 2. He thinks it's pretty.

_____

_____ 3. He has to drive to work.

_____

_____ 4. It's ten miles to his work.

_____

_____ 5. They say it's not going to snow much.

_____

_____ 6. Driving will be dangerous.

_____

II. Word Review

Complete the sentences with these words.

so	how	inches	about
begin	dangerous	hate	far

1. It's very _____ to drink and drive.

2. I walk to school every day. It's not _____.

3. This paper is eight and a half _____ wide.

4–5. When does the play _____? And _____ long is it?

6. It's _____ two hours long.

7–8. I _____ to drive with Angela. She drives _____ fast.

No School Tomorrow

Listen to and pronounce these words.

Nouns	**Verbs**	**Other**
snowball	mean	wet
fight	shovel	

Complete the dialogue with these words and practice it with your partner.

fights   shovel   still   wet   of course   means

Ricky: Is it _____ snowing hard?

Dean: Yes, we have almost six inches.

Ricky: You know what that _____.

Dean: Yes, driving will be difficult.

Ricky: And there'll be a lot of snow to _____.

Dean: But the kids will be happy.

Ricky: That's right. There'll be no school tomorrow.

Dean: And the snow is very _____.

Ricky: So it'll be perfect for snowball _____.

Dean: And for making snow men.

Ricky: Or snow women.

Dean: _____.

Interviewing

Ask your partner or some other person these questions.

1. May I ask you some questions?

2. Why is jogging good for our health?

3. Do you get much exercise?

4. What kind of exercise do you get?

5. How often do you take a nap? Frequently? Sometimes? Rarely? Never?

6. Are you afraid to drive in the snow?

7. How far do you have to go to get to work (school)?

8. How do you get to work (school)?

When Do We Usually Wear It?

*Next to each word, write **hot** if we usually wear this clothing in hot weather. Write **cold** if we usually wear it when it's cold.*

1. gloves   _____

2. shorts   _____

3. boots   _____

4. tee shirt   _____

5. scarf   _____

6. hat   _____

7. swim suit   _____

8. long underwear _____

Review

Reread the story **From Santiago to New York** *(page 120 of* **The Pizza Tastes Great***) before doing the story, word, and word and story reviews.*

I. Story Review

If the sentence is true, write **T**. *If it's false, write* **F** *and change it to a true statement.*

_____ 1. Sandra comes from Santiago, a city in the Dominican Republic.

_____

_____ 2. She lives in Manhattan with her parents.

_____

_____ 3. Her brothers want to stay in the Dominican Republic.

_____

_____ 4. She works in her cousin's grocery store.

_____

_____ 5. She works long hours, and her job is difficult.

_____

_____ 6. She doesn't know any English.

_____

_____ 7. Americans seem cold to Sandra.

_____

_____ 8. She's going to go back to Santiago.

_____

II. Word Review

Complete the sentences with these words.

if	crying	friendly	have to
almost	dream	sometimes	seems

1. Dinner is _____ ready.

2-3. Erica _____ to be a very nice person. She's very _____, and I like her a lot.

4. In the winter, I _____ of warm weather.

5. Tim will help us _____ we ask him.

6. _____ we play ping-pong after school.

7. Wait here. I _____ put my books in my locker.

8. The baby is _____. I think she's hungry.

III. Word and Story Review

No Jobs There for Me

Carlos meets Sandra at a party, and they're talking.

Complete the conversation with these words and practice it with your partner.

there are	**uncle**	**still**	**grocery**
until	**stay**	**owns**	**go back**

Carlos: Where do you work, Sandra?

Sandra: In a _____ store on Broadway.

Carlos: Do you like your work?

Sandra: No. The hours are too long.

Carlos: What are they?

Sandra: I work from ten in the morning _____ eight at night.

Carlos: Wow! That is long. Who _____ the store?

Sandra: My cousin.

Carlos: And where do you live?

Sandra: In an apartment with my _____ and cousins.

Carlos: Are your parents _____ in the Dominican Republic?

Sandra: Yes, they live in Santiago.

Carlos: Do they want to come to New York?

Sandra: No, they want to _____ in Santiago.

Carlos: How do you like New York?

Sandra: I don't. I want to _____ to Santiago.

Carlos: Well, why don't you?

Sandra: _____ no jobs there for me.

What a Difference!

Read and enjoy the story about Juan. Then write a similar story about a person's first year in the United States.

Juan is sixteen, and he comes from Lima, the capital of Peru. He lives with his dad and older brother in a small apartment in Philadelphia. He goes to a large public high school. His mom and younger sister still live in Lima, but they're coming to Philadelphia next year. He can't wait to see them again.

At first, Juan didn't like it in Philadelphia. He didn't know anyone at school. He didn't understand English, and the snow and cold were terrible. And of course he missed his mom, his sister, and all of his friends.

Now it's a year later, and he feels at home in Philadelphia. He has a lot of friends at school. He's getting A's in math and science and B's in English and history. He's one of the best players on the soccer team. His dream is to go to college and become an accountant, and his teachers say he can do it. He's happy. What a difference a year makes!

My First Year in the United States

Write a story about your or another person's first year in the United States.

_____

_____

_____

_____

_____

_____

_____

_____

_____

_____

_____

_____

_____

_____

_____

_____

Review

*Reread the story **Sandra Can't Wait** (page 123 of **The Pizza Tastes Great**) before doing the story, word, and word and story reviews.*

I. Story Review

*If the sentence is true, write **T**. If it's false, write **F** and change it to a true statement.*

_____ 1. Sandra likes many things about living in the United States.

_____

_____ 2. She sends her parents a money order every week.

_____

_____ 3. Her uncle is teaching her how to drive.

_____

_____ 4. Roberto is a year older than Sandra.

_____

_____ 5. Sandra and Roberto plan to get married in June.

_____

_____ 6. She reads his letters three or four times and saves them.

_____

_____ 7. Taxis are expensive in Santiago.

_____

_____ 8. Roberto plans to come to the United States soon.

_____

II. Word Review

Complete the sentences with these words.

sending	money order	yet	times
every	arrive	answer	cost

1. How many _____ do I have to tell you to clean your room?

2-3. When is the president going to _____? We're not sure. He isn't here _____.

4. Mark is _____ his girlfriend a dozen roses for Valentine's Day.

5. I have some mail I have to _____.

6. I want a _____ for a hundred dollars, please.

7. Gina visits her mother _____ Friday.

8. I'm going to buy this ring if it doesn't _____ too much.

III. Word and Story Review

What Do You Like?

Carlos meets Sandra at a party, and they're talking.

Complete the conversation with these words and practice it with your partner.

soon	department stores	get married	save
shop	visa	beach	also

Carlos: What do you like about living in the United States?

Sandra: I can _____ money.

Carlos: What else do you like?

Sandra: I like to _____ here.

Carlos: Where do you usually shop?

Sandra: In the big _____.

Carlos: Me too. They have everything.

Sandra: And in the summer, I like to go to the _____.

Carlos: I'm sure that's fun.

Sandra: It is, and I'm _____ learning to drive.

Carlos: Do you have a boyfriend?

Sandra: Yes. His name is Roberto. We're going to _____.

Carlos: Does he live in New York?

Sandra: No, in Santiago, but he's coming here _____.

Carlos: That's great!

Sandra: Yes. He's waiting for his _____.

Carlos: It was nice talking to you. Good luck!

Sandra: Thanks.

Matching

In front of the words in column A, print the capital letters that are next to their definitions or descriptions in column B.

	Column A	Column B
_____	1. mine	A. a good place to go in the summer
_____	2. leaves	B. the one after this
_____	3. wear	C. there are four
_____	4. inches	D. we need them to send letters
_____	5. beach	E. want to
_____	6. impossible	F. trees have lots of them
_____	7. stamps	G. my mother's sister
_____	8. next	H. we do this with clothing
_____	9. temperature	I. can't be
_____	10. would like	J. what I own
_____	11. seasons	K. how hot or cold it is
_____	12. aunt	L. most rulers have twelve

Talking It Over

Discuss these questions with another student or in a small group.

1. If you are working, what time do you begin work? And what time do you finish?

2. Where can people get jobs if they don't know English?

3. Do you have a dream—something you really want to be or to have? What is it?

4. Are you able to save money?

5. Name some big department stores.

6. Why is it expensive to own a car?

7. Does a person have to wait long for a visa?

8. Do you usually write to relatives in your first country, or do you phone them?

7

Sports and Fun

Review

Reread the dialogue **A House at the Shore** *(page 129 of* **The Pizza Tastes Great***) before doing the dialogue and word reviews.*

I. Dialogue Review

If the sentence is true, write **T**. *If it's false, write* **F** *and change it to a true statement.*

_____   1. Fran's vacation begins next week.

   _____

_____   2. He's buying a house at the shore.

   _____

_____   3. Fran and his wife like the ocean.

   _____

_____   4. They swim in the ocean a lot.

   _____

_____   5. Chris asks why they're going to the shore.

   _____

_____   6. Fran says they love to walk on the beach.

   _____

II. Word Review

Complete the sentences with these words.

start	**wonderful**	**renting**	**vacation**
shore	**lie on**	**then**	**next**

1. Sal likes to _____ the sofa and listen to music.

2. We're _____ some chairs and tables for the party.

3-4. I live a mile from the _____. _____ why don't you go to the beach in the summer?

5. My daughter is five. She's going to _____ school this month.

6. When is the _____ plane to San Francisco?

7. I think it's _____ that you're helping Peter.

8. We're going to Florida on our _____.

Missing Lines

Use the following lines to complete the miniconversations.

Be careful! Too much sun isn't good for you.   How long is your vacation?
Sure! I love to swim.   Do you travel a lot?
Are you going to rent that apartment?

1. **Lee:** _____

   Dean: No, it's too small.

2. **Lee:** I'm going to lie on the beach this afternoon.

   Dean: _____

3. **Lee:** _____

   Dean: No, not very much.

4. **Lee:** _____

   Dean: Three weeks.

5. **Lee:** Do you want to go to the shore with me?

   Dean: _____

Washington in September

Listen to and pronounce these words.

Nouns	Verb	Other
middle	hope	away
museum		so

Complete the dialogue with these words and practice it with your partner.

museums flying middle away so weather

Kelly: When are you taking your vacation?

Robin: Not until the _____ of September.

Kelly: Why so late?

Robin: I like the _____ in September.

Kelly: Are you going _____?

Robin: Yes, to Washington, D.C.

Kelly: What are you going to visit?

Robin: The White House, the _____, a lot of places.

Kelly: Maybe you'll see the president.

Robin: I hope _____.

Kelly: Are you _____?

Robin: No, we're taking the train.

Writing a Dialogue

Work with a partner and create your own dialogue. Use the words in this lesson and other words you know.

_____

A: When is your vacation?

B: _____

A: Where are you going?

B: _____

A: _____

B: _____

A: _____

B: _____

Vacations and Renting

Discuss these questions with another student or in a small group.

1. Can you tell us a little about your last vacation?

2. When is your next vacation?

3. How long will it be?

4. Do you have any plans for it? If you do, what are they?

5. List four things people often rent.

    A. _____

    B. _____

    C. _____

    D. _____

6. Why do people rent things?

Review

Reread the dialogue **A Picnic** *(page 132 of* **The Pizza Tastes Great***) before doing the dialogue and word reviews.*

I. Dialogue Review

If the sentence is true, write **T**. *If it's false, write* **F** *and change it to a true statement.*

_____   1. Pat wants to go to a baseball game.

_____

_____   2. Pat and Gerry are going to a park.

_____

_____   3. It's about three miles to the park.

_____

_____   4. The park has picnic tables and a pretty lake.

_____

_____   5. They're going to bring soda, cookies, and sandwiches.

_____

_____   6. The kids won't want to go.

_____

II. Word Review

Complete the sentences with these words.

shall	**great**	**beautiful**	**let's**
kids	**about**	**bring**	**far**

1. Is the airport _____ from here?

2. I love your garden. It's very _____.

3–4. Where are the _____? Why didn't you _____ them with you?

5. New York and Paris are _____ cities to visit.

6. It's eleven o'clock and I'm tired. _____ go home.

7. _____ a million people live in Dallas, Texas.

8. I'm very hungry. Where _____ we eat lunch?

Bear Mountain State Park

Listen to and pronounce these words.

Nouns		**Verbs**	**Other**
hike*	pool	hike	less (than)
zoo		get = arrive	

Complete the dialogue with these words and practice it with your partner.

zoo　　　**less**　　　**hike**　　　**get**　　　**how about**　　　**pool**

Gita: What do you want to do on Saturday?

Raj: I don't know.

Gita: Let's go for a _____ with the kids.

Raj: That's a wonderful idea! Where shall we go?

Gita: _____ Bear Mountain State Park?

Raj: Perfect. It has a lot of places to hike.

Gita: And a _____.

Raj: Great! The kids will love the animals.

Gita: And it has a swimming _____.

Raj: How long will it take to _____ there?

Gita: _____ than an hour. It's about fifty miles.

Raj: Good. That's not so far.

*A **hike** is a long walk.

125

Interviewing

Ask your partner or some other person these questions.

1. May I ask you some questions?

2. When you go away on a vacation, who do you usually go with?

3. Did you ever visit Washington, D.C.? If you did, what did you see?

4. Do you like to travel by train?

5. Do you like to hike—to go for long walks?

6. Do you hike much?

7. Do you like to visit zoos?

8. Do you think it's best to swim in a pool, in a lake, or in the ocean?

Picnics and Parks

A. List four or five things people often take on a picnic. Work with a partner.

1. _____

2. _____

3. _____

4. _____

5. _____

B. List four or five things people often do on a picnic.

1. _____

2. _____

3. _____

4. _____

5. _____

C. Discuss these questions with your partner.

1. Do you like sandwiches?

2. What kind you like?

3. What is your favorite soda?

4. Do you drink a lot of soda?

5. Is there a park near your house or apartment?

6. Do you use it much?

Review

Reread the dialogue **I'm Going Skiing** *(page 135 of* **The Pizza Tastes Great***) before doing the dialogue and word reviews.*

I. Dialogue Review

If the sentence is true, write **T**. *If it's false, write* **F** *and change it to a true statement.*

_____ 1. Terry is unhappy about the snow.

_____

_____ 2. Terry likes to ski.

_____

_____ 3. Carol wants to go skiing with Terry.

_____

_____ 4. Terry says it's safe to drive.

_____

_____ 5. Carol compares driving and skiing.

_____

_____ 6. Terry tells Carol not to worry.

_____

II. Word Review

Complete the sentences with these words.

fun	careful	worry	maybe
terrific	has got	too	dangerous

1. _____ Sam can help us. I'll ask him.

2. Jennifer _____ a bad headache.

3. Danielle doesn't look well. I _____ about her.

4. Jason is the fastest swimmer in the school. He's _____!

5. The park is pretty, but it's _____ at night.

6. I like to read. It's _____.

7. Brenda is a lawyer, and her husband is _____.

8. Be _____! The floor is wet.

Missing Lines

Use the following lines to complete the miniconversations.

Playing in the street is dangerous.   It's a lot of fun. I love it.
My husband is in the hospital.   Are you serious?
I got a hundred on my history test.

1. **Pat:** _____

   Lee: Don't worry. He'll be okay.

2. **Pat:** Why do you ski so much?

   Lee: _____

3. **Pat:** _____

   Lee: That's why the children should go to the park.

4. **Pat:** I'm having lunch with the president of the United States.

   Lee: _____

5. **Pat:** _____

   Lee: Wow! That's terrific!

Can You Ice-Skate?

Listen to and pronounce these words.

Nouns	Verb	Other
hockey	ice-skate	rough
skater		

Complete the dialogue with these words and practice it with your partner.

safe	degrees	hockey	ice-skate	rough	sounds

Jan: It's twenty _____ out.

Pete: Great!

Jan: What so great about it?

Pete: I'll be able to _____ on the lake.

Jan: That _____ like fun.

Pete: It is. Can you skate?

Jan: A little.

Pete: Why don't you come with me?

Jan: Okay. Do you think the ice is _____?

Pete: It must be by now.

Jan: I hope you're right. Are you a good skater?

Pete: Yes, I'm on the _____ team.

Jan: That's a _____ sport.

Pete: I know, but I love it.

Writing a Dialogue

Work with a partner and create your own dialogue. Use the words in this lesson and other words you know.

_____

A: It's going to be hot today.

B: That's good!

A: What's so good about it?

B: I _____ .

A: _____

B: _____

A: _____

B: _____

Sentence Completion

Complete these sentences.

1. I **have got** _____ .

2. **Maybe** I should _____ .

3. I'm not a **terrific** _____ , but I _____ .

4. _____ and I do **too.**

5. I'm **careful** when I _____ .

6. Ice hockey is a **rough** sport. _____ and _____ are also rough sports.

7. _____ and _____ aren't rough sports.

Review

Reread the dialogue **A Soccer Game** *(page 138 of* **The Pizza Tastes Great***) before doing the dialogue and word reviews.*

I. Dialogue Review

If the sentence is true, write **T**. *If it's false, write* **F** *and change it to a true statement.*

_____ 1. Sandy is going to play soccer.

_____

_____ 2. He's going to play with his cousins.

_____

_____ 3. He's the best player on the team.

_____

_____ 4. The game starts at ten o'clock.

_____

_____ 5. Lynn is going to watch Sandy play.

_____

_____ 6. She wants Sandy's team to win.

_____

II. Word Review

Complete the sentences with these words.

hope	team	best	win
soccer	later	begins	busy

1. School _____ again in September.

2. I _____ you get the job.

3. We have a meeting now. I'll talk to you _____.

4. Joan is so _____ she doesn't have time for lunch.

5–6. How good is the basketball _____ this year? Very good. We

should _____ most of our games.

7. In _____, you move the ball with your feet, not your hands.

8. This is the _____ Italian restaurant in the area.

Come On! You'll Feel Better!

Listen to and pronounce these words.

Nouns		**Verbs**	**Other**
exercise	pace	come on	long
excuse	shape		

Complete the dialogue with these words and practice it with your partner.

exercise   who's   excuses   shape   other   pace

Casey: Where are you going?

Kyle: For a long walk.

Casey: How often do you go for a walk?

Kyle: Every _____ day.

Casey: I should get more _____.

Kyle: Why don't you come with me?

Casey: I'm busy.

Kyle: No _____! Come on! You'll feel better!

Casey: How far do you walk?

Kyle: Three miles at a fast _____.

Casey: You must be in good _____.

Kyle: I am, for someone _____ sixty.

Casey: Okay, I'll go with you.

Kyle: Good. You can finish your work later.

Interviewing

Ask your partner or some other person these questions.

1. May I ask you some questions?

2. Can you ice-skate? Do you ice-skate much?

3. Do you like ice hockey?

4. Do you ever watch hockey on TV? Do you watch it much?

5. Hockey and football are dangerous sports. Which do you think is more dangerous?

6. Can you name two countries (not counting the United States) in which hockey is very popular?

7. Do you like to go for walks?

8. Do you walk much?

What Can You Do (Well)?

Name three or four things you can do. If you can do them well, put a check between the parentheses (√).

1. I can _____. ( )

2. I can _____. ( )

3. I can _____. ( )

4. I can _____. ( )

Name three things you can't do. If you want to learn how to do them, put a check between the parentheses.

1. I can't _____. ( )

2. I can't _____. ( )

3. I can't _____. ( )

Review

Reread the story **Peace and Quiet** *(page 141 of* **The Pizza Tastes Great***) before doing the story, word, and word and story reviews.*

I. Story Review

If the sentence is true, write **T**. *If it's false, write* **F** *and change it to a true statement.*

_____   1. Harry and Nancy are going away for a week.

_____

_____   2. They're renting a house on a lake north of Miami.

_____

_____   3. They're leaving tonight.

_____

_____   4. Harry's a carpenter, but he doesn't like his job.

_____

_____   5. He enjoys the peace and quiet of the country.

_____

_____   6. Nancy and Harry like to fish.

_____

_____   7. Nancy is an excellent swimmer.

_____

_____   8. She spends a lot of time taking people to look at houses.

_____

II. Word Review

Complete the sentences with these words.

building	country	often	spends
quiet	repairing	peace	excellent

1. The United Nations helps countries live in _____.

2. The college is _____ a new library.

3. How _____ do you go to the movies?

4. Mr. Morales is a (an) _____ history teacher.

5. Hillary is looking for a _____ place to read.

6. The children like to look at the cows and horses when they go to the _____.

7. Melissa _____ hours practicing the piano.

8. Gary is _____ his boat. It's getting old.

III. Word and Story Review

Going on Vacation

Nancy is talking to her brother Ralph.

Complete the conversation with these words and practice it with your partner.

sell	enjoy	leaving	real estate
relax	packing	carpenter	feeling

Ralph: Why are you _____ your clothes?

Nancy: We're going on vacation.

Ralph: Where are you going?

Nancy: To a lake a hundred miles north of Miami.

Ralph: When are you _____?

Nancy: Tomorrow morning at nine.

Ralph: It must be a great _____.

Nancy: Yes, it'll be nice to go swimming and to _____.

Ralph: How is your _____ business?

Nancy: Fine, I love to _____ houses, but I need a break.

Ralph: I can imagine. What's Harry doing?

Nancy: He's working in the _____ shop.

Ralph: Give him my best, and _____ your vacation!

Nancy: Thanks, we will.

Going to California

Read and enjoy the story about Steve and Helen. Then write a similar story about a couple going on a vacation.

Steve and Helen are at JFK (John F. Kennedy) Airport in New York City. They're going to California for two weeks, and they're going to stay with Helen's sister, who lives in San Diego. This is their first trip to California, and they're excited. Their plane is going to take off in an hour.

Steve works for the United Parcel Service (UPS). He drives a truck and delivers packages. He likes his job, but he doesn't like to drive in the snow. His salary isn't great, but it's not bad either.

Helen works for a travel agency in New York City. She helps people arrange their vacations and other trips. She's friendly and likes to work with people. She knows the best places to go for a vacation, and she's good at making reservations at hotels and on the airlines. Because of her work, she was able to get free tickets for their trip to California.

A Couple Going on a Vacation

Write a story similar to **Going to California,** *or write one about any person or persons.*

_____

_____

_____

_____

_____

_____

_____

_____

_____

_____

_____

_____

_____

_____

_____

Review

Reread the story **No Children This Year** *(page 144 of* **The Pizza Tastes Great***) before doing the story, word, and word and story reviews.*

I. Story Review

If the sentence is true, write **T**. *If it's false, write* **F** *and change it to a true statement.*

_____ 1. Nancy and Harry's children are going on vacation with them.

_____

_____ 2. Their son is away at college.

_____

_____ 3. They feel a little lonely without their children.

_____

_____ 4. Harry can't cook, but he helps with the dishes.

_____

_____ 5. After Nancy and Harry do the dishes, they go for a walk.

_____

_____ 6. They usually sleep late in the morning.

_____

_____ 7. They walk to the state park, which is not far from their house.

_____

_____ 8. The trees in the park are pretty.

_____

II. Word Review

Complete the sentences with these words.

lonely	**usually**	**noise**	**be able**
forgets	**without**	**stay up**	**together**

1. I'm too tired to _____ tonight.

2. My daughter sometimes feels _____ when she's away at camp, but she has fun.

3–4. Will you _____ to go to the movies tonight? I don't want to go _____ you.

5. The dishwasher is making a lot of _____.

6–7. Frank and I like to jog _____. We _____ jog after work.

8. Beth sometimes _____ to brush her teeth before she goes to bed.

III. Word and Story Review

Swimming and Fishing

Complete the conversation with these words and practice it with your partner.

woods	couple	heat	long
away from	few	both	fresh

Nancy: It's great to get _____ the real estate office.

Harry: And the _____ of Miami.

Nancy: Yes, and the air here is _____.

Harry: And the lake is so pretty.

Nancy: What shall we do today?

Harry: Let's go for a walk in the _____.

Nancy: Perfect. The state park is only a _____ miles from here.

Harry: I love _____ walks in the park.

Nancy: And tonight we can play cards with the _____ next door.

Harry: Fine. We _____ like to play cards.

Nancy: Tomorrow I'm going swimming.

Harry: And I'm going fishing.

Nancy: This is going to be a wonderful vacation.

Harry: I think so, too.

Matching

In front of the words in column A, print the capital letters that are next to their definitions or descriptions in column B.

	Column A	Column B
_____	1. swimming	A. what many eat for lunch
_____	2. rent	B. you need snow to do this
_____	3. zoo	C. works with wood
_____	4. dishes	D. children
_____	5. ski	E. to pay to use
_____	6. shore	F. a game we play on ice
_____	7. carpenter	G. a long walk
_____	8. hockey	H. what we use to eat dinner
_____	9. vacation	I. fish are good at this
_____	10. kids	J. where the ocean meets land
_____	11. hike	K. a time to rest and have fun
_____	12. sandwiches	L. a place to see animals

Talking It Over

Discuss these questions with another student or in a small group.

1. Do you think you're a hard worker?

2. Is it easy for you to relax?

3. What do you do to relax?

4. Do you live in a city? Do you like living there? Explain your answer.

5. Which do you like better? The peace and quiet of the country, or the activity of a city?

6. Do you like to read when you're on vacation?

7. Do you like to sleep late when you're on vacation?

8

Schools and Children

Review

Reread the dialogue **Is English Difficult?** *(page 150 of* **The Pizza Tastes Great***) before doing the dialogue and word reviews.*

I. Dialogue Review

If the sentence is true, write **T**. *If it's false, write* **F** *and change it to a true statement.*

_____ 1. Fran is going to work.

_____

_____ 2. He's Polish.

_____

_____ 3. He thinks English is easy.

_____

_____ 4. He has to study a lot.

_____

_____ 5. He's far from his school.

_____

_____ 6. He likes his class.

_____

II. Word Review

Complete the sentences with these words.

fun	difficult	learning	kind
blocks	a lot	have to	practices

1. We can walk to the park. It's only five _____.

2–4. Audrey is _____ to use a computer. She _____

typing on the computer every day. She wants to be a secretary, and secretaries

use computers _____.

5. Ivan likes to go fishing. It's _____.

6–7. You don't _____ be afraid of Mr. Roberts. He's very

_____.

8. Pam is studying to be a lawyer. It's _____.

Missing Lines

Use the following lines to complete the miniconversations.

Why not?　　　　　　　　　　I have to study for my science test.
That's good. Was Brian there?　Do you speak English?
Where are you going?

1. **Pat:** _____

   Terry: To the movies.

2. **Pat:** I don't like my teacher.

   Terry: _____

3. **Pat:** _____

   Terry: No, I'm from Mexico.

4. **Pat:** The party was a lot of fun.

   Terry: _____

5. **Pat:** _____

   Terry: When is it?

Stay in School

142

Listen to and pronounce these words.

Nouns		**Verb**	**Other**
weekend	diploma	quit	full-time
rest		hire	

Complete the dialogue with these words and practice it with your partner.

let	**rest**	**weekends**	**hire**	**diploma**	**quit**

Juan: Mom, I want to get a job.

Mom: On _____?

Juan: No, I want a full-time job, five days a week.

Mom: What about school?

Juan: I want to _____.

Mom: I won't _____ you.

Juan: Why not?

Mom: Who's going to _____ you?

Juan: McDonald's.

Mom: Do you want to work there for the _____ of your life?

Juan: Of course not.

Mom: Then stay in school and get a _____.

Writing a Dialogue

Work with a partner and create your own dialogue. Use the words in this lesson and other words you know.

_____

A: What school are you going to?

B: To _____.

A: What country are you from?

B: _____

A: _____

B: _____

A: _____

B: _____

School and Work

Discuss these questions with another student or in a small group.

1. Do (did) you like school?

2. Why do (did) you like school? Or why don't (didn't) you like school?

3. Do you think it's easy to get a job without a high school diploma? Explain your answer.

4. If you go to school, do you also work?

5. If you go to school and work, do you like working?

6. Does working make school more difficult? Explain your answer.

Review

*Reread the dialogue **A Lazy Boy** (page 153 of **The Pizza Tastes Great**) before doing the dialogue and word reviews.*

I. Dialogue Review

*If the sentence is true, write **T**. If it's false, write **F** and change it to a true statement.*

_____   1. Terry is angry at Jim's teachers.

_____

_____   2. Jim is doing well in school.

_____

_____   3. Jackie thinks Jim is smart.

_____

_____   4. Jim studies a lot.

_____

_____   5. His teachers say he's nice, but very lazy.

_____

_____   6. Terry is afraid his teachers are right.

_____

II. Word Review

Complete the sentences with these words.

so	**surprise**	**smart**	**afraid**
angry	**well**	**maybe**	**lazy**

1. Mr. Roberts is a good teacher, but he gets _____ a lot.

2. When I don't understand my homework, I ask Sara for help. She's _____.

3. Frank likes to sing, and he sings _____.

4. I was _____ today. I didn't do any work.

5. Karen is very pretty. Don't you think _____?

6. Don't be _____ to ask questions. That's how you learn.

7. It's a nice day. _____ I'll go for a walk after work. I'm not sure yet.

8. The teacher didn't tell the students about the test. She wanted it to be a _____.

History Is Important

Listen to and pronounce these words.

Nouns		**Verbs**	**Other**
history	past	behave	enough
trouble	mistake	fail	boring

Complete the dialogue with these words and practice it with your partner.

past   **behaving**   **enough**   **mistakes**   **failing**   **boring**

Pat: My history teacher wants to see you.

Dad: If you're not _____, you're in trouble.

Pat: That's not the problem.

Dad: Well, what is?

Pat: I'm _____ history.

Dad: Are you studying?

Pat: Sometimes.

Dad: That's not good _____.

Pat: But I think history is _____.

Dad: Maybe it is, but it's very important.

Pat: Why?

Dad: We learn from the _____.

Pat: What?

Dad: Not to make the same _____.

Interviewing

Ask your partner or some other person these questions.

1. May I ask you some questions?

2. Do you think English is a difficult language? If so, why?

3. It's very difficult for an adult to learn a second language. Why?

4. Is it good to know two languages, to be bilingual? Explain your answer.

5. Do you think history is interesting or boring? Explain your answer.

6. Are you studying history now? If so, are you studying American history or world history?

7. Do you know much about American history?

8. Do you think you should study more? Or do you study enough?

Which Subjects Do You Like?

List the subjects you're studying in school. Then circle a number next to the subject to show how much you like that subject.

1 = I like the subject a lot.

2 = I like the subject.

3 = I dislike the subject. (I dislike means I don't like.)

4 = I dislike the subject a lot.

Subjects

A. _____	1	2	3	4
B. _____	1	2	3	4
C. _____	1	2	3	4
D. _____	1	2	3	4
E. _____	1	2	3	4
F. _____	1	2	3	4
G. _____	1	2	3	4

Review

Reread the dialogue **Not So Young** *(page 156 of* **The Pizza Tastes Great***) before doing the dialogue and word reviews.*

I. Dialogue Review

If the sentence is true, write **T**. *If it's false, write* **F** *and change it to a true statement.*

_____ 1. Carol's son is graduating from college.

_____

_____ 2. Sandy's daughter is nineteen.

_____

_____ 3. Carol remembers when Sandy's daughter was a baby.

_____

_____ 4. Sandy says he and Carol are young.

_____

_____ 5. Carol was young when she got married.

_____

_____ 6. Carol and Sandy aren't so young now.

_____

II. Word Review

Complete the sentences with these words.

graduated	so	get	next
how	remember	get married	young

1. I want to call Ken, but I don't _____ his phone number.

2. When is the _____ train to Washington, D.C.?

3. Stan and Barbara are in love. They plan to _____ in September.

4. I like these flowers. They're _____ pretty.

5. _____ big is the table?

6–7. Our new science teacher is very _____. She _____ from college in June.

8. No one wants to _____ old.

Missing Lines

Use the following lines to complete the miniconversations.

How old are you going to be on Sunday?
Does he have a job yet?
I think that's too young.

I'm getting tired.
When's your birthday?

1. **Robin:** _____

   Leslie: Why don't you go to bed?

2. **Robin:** Greg is graduating from college next week.

   Leslie: _____

3. **Robin:** _____

   Leslie: Two weeks from today.

4. **Robin:** _____

   Leslie: Fifty, but I still feel young.

5. **Robin:** Shirley was seventeen when she got married.

   Leslie: _____

That Makes Me Feel Old

Listen to and pronounce these words.

Noun	Verbs	Other	
grade	believe	whose	taller (than)
	fly (flies)	ninth	anymore

Complete the dialogue with these words and practice it with your partner.

believe	ninth	whose	flies	taller	yet

Jamie: _____ birthday cake is that?

Lynn: My son's.

Jamie: How old is he?

Lynn: Fifteen.

Jamie: Fifteen! I can't _____ it.

Lynn: Well, he is. Time _____.

Jamie: Is he in high school _____?

Lynn: Yes, he's in the _____ grade.

Jamie: I remember the day he was born.

Lynn: And now he's_____ than I am.

Jamie: That makes me feel old.

Lynn: Well, we're not so young anymore.

Jamie: You're right.

Writing a Dialogue

Work with a partner and create your own dialogue. Use the words in this lesson and other words you know.

_____

A: Whose birthday cake is that?

B: _____

A: How old is _____? (he) (she)

B: _____

A: _____

B: _____

A: _____

B: _____

How Much Education Is Necessary?

Circle how much education you think is necessary for these jobs.

       1 = no formal education necessary, but one must be able to do the job

       2 = high school

       3 = college

       4 = college plus

A. teacher	1	2	3	4
B. bus driver	1	2	3	4
C. secretary	1	2	3	4
D. lawyer	1	2	3	4
E. carpenter	1	2	3	4
F. police officer	1	2	3	4

Review

Reread the dialogue **What's a Grant?** *(page 159 of* **The Pizza Tastes Great***) before doing the dialogue and word reviews.*

I. Dialogue Review

If the sentence is true, write **T**. *If it's false, write* **F** *and change it to a true statement.*

_____ 1. It costs a lot to go to college.

_____

_____ 2. Lee's daughter has a grant.

_____

_____ 3. The grant is paying for everything she needs to go to college.

_____

_____ 4. Lee's daughter has a loan.

_____

_____ 5. There's no difference between a loan and a grant.

_____

_____ 6. You have to pay back a grant.

_____

II. Word Review

Complete the sentences with these words.

grant	pay back	great	difference
government	must	loan	expensive

1. I want to go to Europe, but it's very _____.

2. Michael Jordan is a _____ basketball player.

3. The children didn't have lunch yet. They _____ be hungry.

4. There's not much _____ between the weather in January and February.

5–6. Jack's father is rich. That's why Jack can't get a _____ to go to college. However, he can get a _____.

7. Some people think our _____ is too big, that it tries to do too much.

8. I'll give you a hundred dollars, but you have to _____ the money.

I Want to Go to College, but . . . .

Listen to and pronounce these words.

Nouns	**Verbs**	**Other**
aid	attend	then
income	depend	financial
guidance counselor	explain	probably

Complete the dialogue with these words and practice it with your partner.

income   explain   financial   depends   guidance   attend

Gale: Are you going to college?

Tracy: I want to, but . . . .

Gale: But what?

Tracy: My parents don't make much money.

Gale: Then you should be able to get _____ aid.

Tracy: Where from?

Gale: The government and the college you _____.

Tracy: Do you mean the government will help me?

Gale: Probably. It _____.

Tracy: On what?

Gale: Family _____.

Tracy: I'm going to talk to my _____ counselor.

Gale: Good. He'll _____ everything.

Interviewing

Ask your partner or some other person these questions.

1. May I ask you some questions?

2. How old are most students when they graduate from high school?

3. Do you think you're very young, young, or not so young?

4. Do people live longer today? If so, why?

5. Do you think that time flies—that it goes quickly?

6. How much do you think it costs to go to a state college for one year? A private college?

7. Do people need more education today than in the past? If so, why?

8. One good reason to go to college is to prepare for a job. Name another reason to go.

True or False

*If you think the statement is true, write **T**. If you think it's false, write **F**.*

_____ 1. Everyone needs a high school diploma to get a job.

_____ 2. People with more education usually make more money.

_____ 3. College is expensive, so you have to be rich to go to college.

_____ 4. You have to be a very good student to get financial aid.

_____ 5. The government helps many students to go to college.

_____ 6. Many students get loans to go to college.

_____ 7. A loan is usually better than a grant.

_____ 8. Many students work part-time to help pay for college.

Review

Reread the story **Long Hours and Hard Work** *(page 162 of* **The Pizza Tastes Great***) before doing the story, word, and word and story reviews.*

I. Story Review

If the sentence is true, write **T***. If it's false, write* **F** *and change it to a true statement.*

_____ 1. Young Woo and Sun Ok have two children and live in Philadelphia.

_____

_____ 2. They own a clothing store.

_____

_____ 3. In Korea, Sun Ok had a job outside of her home.

_____

_____ 4. Young Woo works hard in the store, but never does any housework.

_____

_____ 5. Sun Ok likes to work in the store.

_____

_____ 6. Young Woo and Sun Ok don't speak English well.

_____

_____ 7. They go to school at night to learn English.

_____

_____ 8. They speak Korean at home.

_____

II. Word Review

Complete the sentences with these words.

hear	housework	almost	change
listening to	never	too	outside

1–2. It's _____ six o'clock, and Janet is cooking dinner and

_____ the radio.

3. Where's the dog? Is she _____?

4. Phil _____ eats meat, but he eats a lot of fish.

5–6. I _____ that you're going to Florida next week. I want to go

_____, but I have to work.

7. Sonia usually drinks coffee, but she's having tea for a _____.

8. Marty doesn't like to do _____, but he's a good cook.

III. Word and Story Review

Is the Store Doing Well?

Young Woo is talking to his friend, Ling Soo.

Complete the conversation with these words and practice it with your partner.

pronounce	hard	own	understand
sell	sounds	close	taking care of

Ling Soo: Good to see you again!

Young Woo: And it's nice to see you!

Ling Soo: How's everything?

Young Woo: Fine. Sun Ok and I _____ a store now.

Ling Soo: What kind of store?

Young Woo: We _____ fruit and vegetables.

Ling Soo: And where's Sun Ok?

Young Woo: She's home; she's _____ the children.

Ling Soo: Is the store doing well?

Young Woo: Very. But it's _____ work.

Ling Soo: You must work long hours.

Young Woo: Yes, we open at eight A.M. and _____ at nine P.M.

Ling Soo: And how's your English?

Young Woo: Better. I _____ everything I hear.

Ling Soo: That's great!

Young Woo: Yes, but English is hard to _____.

Ling Soo: I know, I still have problems with the **l** and the **r** _____.

Akira and Mariko

Read and enjoy the story about Akira and Mariko. Then write a similar story about a family coming to live in the United States.

Akira and Mariko are married and have two children, Kenji and Yoko. They're from Japan and live in Fort Lee, New Jersey. Their home is only a few minutes from the George Washington Bridge. Akira is the supervisor of the loan department in a bank in Fort Lee. Many of the people who use the bank are Japanese. Akira has an accent, but he speaks English very well.

   Mariko stays home and takes care of Kenji and Yoko. Kenji is eight and in the third grade. He loves school and does very well, especially in science. He also loves computers and all kinds of electronic games like Nitendo. On Saturday he goes to a special school where he learns to read and write Japanese. Some day the family may return to Japan, and Kenji wants to know Japanese well.

   Yoko is only three years old, but she goes to a nursery school three days a week. She likes to draw and to paint and to play with her friends. She speaks Japanese at home and English at the nursery school. She's already bilingual.

Living in the United States

Write a story similar to **Akira and Mariko,** *or write a story about any person or persons.*

_____

_____

_____

_____

_____

_____

_____

_____

_____

_____

_____

_____

_____

Review

Reread the story **Excellent Students** *(page 165 of* **The Pizza Tastes Great***) before doing the story, word, and word and story reviews.*

I. Story Review

If the sentence is true, write **T**. *If it's false, write* **F** *and change it to a true statement.*

_____ 1. Schools in the United States and Korea are almost the same.

_____

_____ 2. In Korea, children write down what the teacher says and study it.

_____

_____ 3. In the United States, teachers seem to let the children do what they want.

_____

_____ 4. Tae Ho and Soo Jin's ideas and feelings are almost completely American.

_____

_____ 5. They learn the Korean language at home.

_____

_____ 6. They are very good students, but they don't like school.

_____

_____ 7. Tae Ho likes to play baseball, but he never helps his parents.

_____

_____ 8. Soo Jin is in the second grade and reads well.

_____

II. Word Review

Complete the sentences with these words.

business	**facts**	**best**	**feelings**
way	**half**	**pay attention**	**ideas**

1–3. Ms. Romano is one of the _____ teachers in the school. She has a

lot of good _____, and the students like the _____

she teaches.

4. I can't answer your question now. I have to study the _____ first.

5. When the president speaks, people _____.

6. Leo is in the real estate _____. He sells houses.

7. It was a difficult test. Only _____ the class passed.

8. Sometimes I can't control my _____.

III. Word and Story Review

Learning a Lot

Young Woo is talking to his friend, Ling Soo.

Complete the conversation with these words and practice it with your partner.

lessons	**worry**	**engineer**	**different**
seem	**excellent**	**respect**	**second**

Ling Soo: How are Tae Ho and Soo Jin doing in school?

Young Woo: Fine. They're _____ students.

Ling Soo: Does Tae Ho still want to be a (an) _____?

Young Woo: Yes, and he does very well in math.

Ling Soo: And how old is Soo Jin?

Young Woo: She's seven and in the _____ grade.

Ling Soo: I know she loves school.

Young Woo: Yes, and she also takes piano _____ every week.

Ling Soo: What do you think of the schools in the United States?

Young Woo: They're very _____.

Ling Soo: How?

Young Woo: In Korea, the children have more _____ for teachers.

Ling Soo: That's right.

Young Woo: In the United States, they _____ to do what they want.

Ling Soo: But your children are learning a lot.

Young Woo: True, but we _____ about them.

Matching

In front of the words in column A, print the capital letters that are next to their definitions or descriptions in column B.

Column A	Column B
_____ 1. diploma	A. what teachers give
_____ 2. quit	B. to act the way we should
_____ 3. boring	C. to think that something is true
_____ 4. hire	D. all that we need
_____ 5. government	E. cleaning, doing dishes, making beds
_____ 6. believe	F. what we get when we graduate
_____ 7. close (verb)	G. to give a job to
_____ 8. housework	H. what we hear
_____ 9. sound	I. not interesting
_____ 10. lessons	J. to shut
_____ 11. enough	K. it runs the country
_____ 12. behave	L. to stop doing something

Talking It Over

Discuss these questions with another student or in a small group.

1. How much housework do you do?

2. Do you think housework is boring?

3. Does watching TV help you to learn English?

4. Do you understand most of what you hear on TV?

5. What language do you usually speak with your friends?

6. Are teachers stricter in your first country or in the United States?

7. Do you think students learn more in school in your first country or in the United States?

8. Do you think parents worry a lot about their children?

Word List

The words used in the sentence and dialogue completion exercises and in the matching exercises are listed below.

A

about 17, 65, 110, 124
across 60
ad 87
afraid 68, 96, 145
again 5
age 43
all 3
all right 56
almost 92, 113, 155
alone 18
a lot 5, 34, 141
a lot of 65
already 93
also 17, 72, 117
always 15, 59
angry 37, 95, 145
anniversary 50
another 6, 33, 85
answer (verb) 55, 116
answer (noun) 71
any 9, 11
anything 46
appetite 75, 76
apply 65, 76
appointment 27
around 83
arrive 116
at night 8
attend 153
aunt 118
awake 8
away 122
away from 138

B

bake 11, 19
bakery 46, 57
be able 137
beach 117, 118
beautiful 124
be back 106
because 17
begin 41, 92, 110, 131
beginning (noun) 40
behave 146, 160
believe 150, 160
belong 36
best 56, 131, 158
better 24, 41, 108
bill 34
bird 104
birthday 43
bit 25
block 141
boring 146, 160
born 36
both 92, 138
brave 52
briefcase 49, 57
bring 124
build 87, 134
business 158
busy 5, 19, 72, 131
buy 18, 19, 106

C

calorie 15
camera 50
can 2
careful 15, 80, 127
carpenter 135, 139
cash 65
change (verb) 55, 103
change (noun) 155
cheap 80
chocolate 9
clear 101
climb 63
close (near) 66
close (shut) 92, 156, 160
closet 97
clothes 18
cold 24
collect 37
collection 36
comfortable 68, 76
company 87
compare 37
completely 96
computer 53
construction 87
cook 2
cooler 99
correct 96, 97
cost 65, 80, 116
count 93
country 134
couple 138
cousin 43, 57
cry 113

D

dangerous   110, 127
daughter   3
degree   103, 129
department stores   34, 117
depend   153
dessert   9
diet   14
difference   152
different   15, 49, 159
difficult   75, 141
dining room   3
dinner   2
diploma   143, 160
dirty   59
dish   139
dream   113
drive   47, 80
due   40

E

early   15, 22, 89
eat   3
eat out   75
either   71
else   46, 57
engineer   159
enjoy   135
enough   146, 160
especially   93
every   24, 52, 116
excellent   12, 72, 134, 159
excited   69
excuse   132
exercise   132
expensive   34, 50, 152
explain   153

F

fact   158
fail   146
fair   71
fall   63
far   66, 110, 124
fast   14
favorite   15, 19, 56, 103
feel   24, 52
feeling   135, 158
fever   27
few   18, 138
fight (verb)   18, 96
fight (noun)   111
file   72, 76
financial   153
find   85
finish   34
first   36
fish   11
fix   72, 87
flu   31
fly (flies)   68, 76, 122, 150
foolish   68
forget   63, 96, 137
fresh   104, 138
friendly   18, 19, 113
full   82, 97
fun   72, 108, 127, 141
future   74

G

garage   63
get (arrive)   46, 125
get (become)   53, 148
get (obtain)   11, 82
get back   57
get in   76
get married   117, 148

get up   89
glad   22, 78
go back   114
God   24
go out   33
got   49
government   152, 160
graduate   34, 148
grant   152
grass   104
great   40, 124, 152
grocery   114
guidance   153

H

half   158
handsome   44, 75
hanger   62
hard   56, 156
has got   127
hate   89, 99, 110
have to, has to,   34, 65, 89, 113, 141
headache   22
hear   21, 41, 155
heat   138
heavy   5, 19, 75, 106
help   31, 60
herself   37
high   63
hike   125, 139
hire   143, 160
hit   96
hobby   37
hockey   129, 139
honey   82
hope (noun)   75
hope (verb)   24, 55, 131
hospital   47
housework   155, 160